MOE BERG

The Spy Behind
Home Plate

MOE BERG

The Spy Behind Home Plate

VIVIAN GREY

THE JEWISH PUBLICATION SOCIETY
Philadelphia • Jerusalem

Photos on pages 22, 24, 27, and 31 provided courtesy of the
Nassau Herald and the Bric-A-Brac, Princeton University
Archives, Department of Rare Books and Special Collections,
Princeton University Libraries.

Library of Congress Cataloging-in-Publication Data
Grey, Vivian.
    Moe Berg, the spy behind home plate / by Vivian Grey.
    p. cm.—(A JPS young biography)
    Includes bibliographical references (p. 163) and index.
    ISBN 0-8276-0586-2 (cloth).—ISBN 0-8276-0620-6 (paper)
    1. Berg, Moe, 1902–1972—Juvenile literature. 2. World War,
1939–1945—Secret service—United States—Juvenile literature.
3. Spies—United States—Biography—Juvenile literature.
4. Baseball players—United States—Biography—Juvenile literature.
I. Title. II. Series: JPS young biography series.
D810.S8B4694   1996
940.54'8673--dc20   96-41504

Designed and typeset by Book Design Studio

Printed by Text Press, Inc.

For Rebecca and Leslie
And for Jacquelyn
With love, always

This book is sponsored in memory of the six million Jews who lost their lives during the Holocaust, to the Munich Eleven, and to all of those whose lives were given prematurely because of the history of their times.

The publication of this book has been made possible thanks to the generosity of Ronald Bleznak, Ron Carner, Allen Fox, Alan Magerman, and Bob Spivak, whose devotion to athletics and Jewish sports has been the mainstay of their lives.

Contents

Acknowledgments

There are always many legends and tall tales about major league players, but Moe Berg was different from all the other sports stars because he was also a secret agent for the United States during World War II.

Moe was a great storyteller who loved to spin an exciting yarn, and perhaps facts faded into fantasy as he described his espionage adventures. Indeed, as I searched out the story of Moe's life, I found both believers and disbelievers concerning his exploits and adventures.

We may never know the full story of this man, who at once loved an audience and at the same time wanted to remain hidden in the shadows. However, we do know that Moe played in the majors for sixteen years, successfully wove together scholarly research, the practice of the law, and the life of a celebrity superstar, and then went on to help the United States obtain important information, which it used in its top-secret atomic bomb program. For all of this, Moe deserves to have his story told to young readers so that they may share an adventure in time together.

All material in this book was taken from official records, sources, books, and interviews.

My research over two years led me to many who generously shared their memories or information with me. I now express formal gratitude for their information and encouragement.

My task was made infinitely easier by John Cummings, head of the New Jersey Collection, Newark Public Library. I owe him a debt of gratitude for his patient cooperation, for taking the time to respond to my myriad questions, for personally going to the library's archives and files to retrieve Berg photographs, and for generally helping me to stay the course. The Berg family was a small and very private group, but John Cummings, through his friendship with Moe's brother, Dr. Samuel Berg, generously shared family stories about Sam and Ethel and Moe and, in doing so, helped me to understand the Bergs better.

I also wish to thank Irwin Berg, Moe's cousin, for his help at the onset of this project. Nicholas Dawidoff's meticulous research in his adult book *The Catcher Was a Spy: The Mysterious Life of Moe Berg*, provided a fine sounding board to substantiate and confirm the bits of information that made up the mosaic of Moe's life.

Thanks are due, also, to the cooperative staffs of the New Jersey Historical Society, Princeton University Class of '23 Historian, and Princeton Alumni Weekly, and the staff of The New York Public Library, Manuscripts and Archives Section of the Rare Books and Manuscripts Division, Moe Berg Papers.

As a native of the Newark, New Jersey area, as a former resident of Princeton, and as a former member of the Princeton University League, I was familiar with both Newark and Princeton, and I hope I was able to convey the flavor of these interesting communities.

I am especially indebted to the authors and editors of the books listed in the Bibliography, from which I obtained background information, factual material, or quotations.

And finally, my thanks to my editor, Bruce Black, who was steady, patient, and sensitive, and who always offered his perceptive and constructive editorial comments with a gentle sense of humor.

Chapter 1

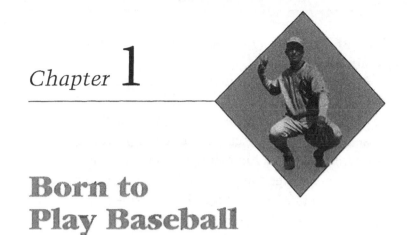

Born to Play Baseball

Ever since Moe Berg could remember, he wanted to play baseball. Moe didn't just want to play after school, or in the sandlot down the street—he wanted to play baseball in the majors. He wanted to make the bat meet the ball and send it soaring over the bleachers. He wanted the whole world to see him hit a home run and have everyone know his name.

But Moe's father, Bernard Berg, did not share his son's passion for baseball and definitely did not want Moe to play it. Moe's father thought that playing baseball was a waste of time that could be better spent studying. Besides, baseball was not a traditional Jewish game. Educated Jews usually didn't become baseball players. According to Bernard Berg, young boys studied hard and grew up to become successful doctors, lawyers, teachers, pharmacists, and businessmen. But not baseball players.

After his father finished telling Moe how much he disliked baseball, he would pull his lips together as if to spit. Only Bernard Berg never spit. He wanted Moe to see how much he scorned baseball players and how little he thought of his youngest son's playing baseball.

With his father's angry scolding ringing in his ears, Moe would take his glove and go outside to play catch in front of his father's drugstore, or he would jog down to the sandlot to meet the team for a game.

He just had to do it. Playing baseball was his whole life.

Chapter 2

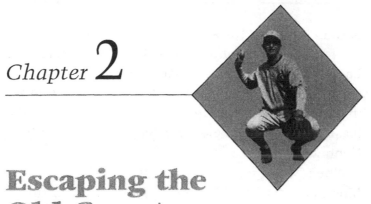

Escaping the Old Country

Moe was born on March 2, 1902 in a New York City tenement on East 121st Street in Harlem, but he grew up in Newark, New Jersey. His real name was Morris, but even as an infant, he was called "Moe."

Moe's parents came to the United States from an area called Kamenets in the Ukraine, Russia. His father's home, Kippinya, was a *shtetl*, a small town, where it was the duty and joy of every Jewish boy to learn and to study.

The Jews of the *shtetl* spoke Yiddish, wrote and read Hebrew, and bargained in broken Polish or Ukrainian. Moe's father Bernard felt cut off and imprisoned in the tiny town. He wanted to learn more about the world outside the *shtetl*. Learning languages was his way of reaching out to the world.

Bernard studied Russian history and philosophy in the public school, and strange-sounding languages— English, French, and German. He also kept up with his religious training. Bernard studied in the morning before school, and in the evenings; he devoted at least one day a week—the Sabbath—to studying Hebrew.

When Moe's father was young and still in school, Moe's grandfather, Mendel Berg, lost several fingers trying to repair a machine. Mendel didn't want his family to receive charity or to be treated as honorable paupers, so the family opened a small tavern and store. At the same time Bernard became a *melamed*, a teacher, and collected tuition from the parents of his students. The money from the business and the money from Bernard's new teaching job held the Berg family together.

When it was time for him to marry, Bernard chose Rose Tasker, who came from a nearby village along the Buy River near Romania. At eighteen, Rose had long dark curly hair, and a small slim figure. She was not pretty in the usual way, with a mouth that was rather too large, and dark brown eyes above wide cheekbones. To Bernard, she had the face of someone who could deal with the best and the worst of what life had to offer.

A year after they met, Rose and Bernard signed the marriage contract and set the wedding date for 1894. But instead of marrying and settling down in the *shtetl* as was expected of them, Rose and Bernard made up their minds to do something daring and different. They postponed their wedding day and changed their lives forever. They were going to America to make a new life.

With twenty dollars, a gift from Rose's father, Bernard had enough money to pay for his passage and to make a start in the new country before sending for Rose. Bernard did not like America at first, so he worked his way back across the Atlantic and tried to settle in England. After searching for a job in London without success, Bernard decided that the United States offered the best chance for a better life after all. Like many other new Jewish immigrants, he moved into a tenement on New York City's crowded Lower East Side.

Bernard first found a job making jewelry boxes. Then he was hired to iron shirts in a laundry. It took him two years to scrape together enough money for Rose's passage across the Atlantic, and the few dollars more they would need to get settled. He sent the money to Rose and asked her to come to America to marry him. Rose's father added a small dowry, gave the couple his blessings, and warned Rose to be careful sneaking out of Russia.

In January of 1897, Rose and Bernard were married in the home of Bernard's cousin, Dr. Danzis of Newark, New Jersey. Dr. Danzis was one of the first Jewish doctors in that city. To Bernard, Dr. Danzis stood for everything American. He was successful, educated, and rich. Best of all, he was a doctor. Bernard hoped and dreamed that one day he would be just like his rich American cousin.

While many other immigrants continued to speak to each other in Yiddish, the language of the old country, Bernard spoke only English. Determined to be an American, he refused to allow anyone to speak anything but English in his home, ever.

Both Rose and Bernard soon realized that learning was the key to success in their new country. They discovered that even America could be like the *shtetl* they had escaped. A good education would help Bernard earn respect, power, and money.

Although Bernard wanted to become a doctor, medical school was too expensive. If he could not become a doctor, he would become a man who gave out medicines, a pharmacist. Bernard signed up for night classes at the New York College of Pharmacy.

But he and Rose had to earn a living while he studied, and so they opened a laundry on Ludlow Street, on New York's lower east side. They were in business for themselves, the first step to prospering in the United States. While they lived behind the laundry, Moe's oldest brother Samuel was born in 1898, followed by his sister Ethel in 1900.

Working and studying and raising a family were sometimes difficult. While Bernard ironed shirts, which took up a lot of time, he studied pharmacy from a book propped up on a book stand. Often he scorched the shirts, and Rose had to take over. Finally, Bernard graduated from the New York College of Pharmacy and passed the New York State Board of Pharmacy exam. He was now a registered pharmacist. At last, he had a real profession.

Soon after, the Bergs sold the laundry and the family moved out to the country, 121st Street in Harlem, to be closer to the drugstore where Bernard now worked. And that was in 1902, when twelve-pound baby Moe was born.

Four years later, in 1906, Bernard and Rose decided to move to Newark, New Jersey, a bustling, growing city. The Bergs would live near Dr. Danzis and their other relatives, and start a business in a city that needed new drugstores.

In 1906, Newark was a patchwork of small connecting towns—Vailsburg, Roseville, Forest Hill, Iron Bound, Clinton Hill, Down Neck, and Weequahic. Each section had its own stores, its own pride, its own way of life, and its own language—Italian, Greek, Irish, German, and Yiddish. Russian, German, and Polish Jews had moved into the Prince Street section with help from their relatives and friends who had arrived earlier. Prince Street became the heart of the Jewish neighborhood, with pushcarts, kosher butcher shops, and chicken and fresh fish markets. Some more adventurous Jews, however, had moved into Newark's outskirts, the Weequahic section.

Bernard and Rose did not want to move to the Weequahic section where most Jews with younger children were settling. Instead, Bernard moved his family to the Roseville section on the opposite side of the city where there were almost no Jews at all. He had run away from the Jewish *shtetl* and wanted a new life for himself and his family.

Roseville was mostly an Irish and Italian neighborhood, with good schools and middle class people who owned their own homes. Bernard bought a newly built corner house with space for a drugstore downstairs and an apartment for the family over the store. Filled with high hopes, the Berg family moved into 92 South Thirteenth Street on the corner of Ninth Avenue. Though Moe would grow up to be a famous ballplayer and would live all over the world, Newark and this Roseville neighborhood would always be his "home plate."

Chapter 3

School Days

It was not easy being Jewish most of the year in the Roseville section of Newark. It was even harder between Thanksgiving and Christmas. For Moe and his brother and sister, Christmas in Roseville meant six weeks of misery added to their year-round feeling that they didn't belong.

As one of the few Jewish families in Roseville, the Bergs were not invited to neighborhood Christmas parties. Almost everyone else belonged to a church, but Moe's parents didn't even go to a synagogue. Because of their father's desire to become American, neither Moe nor his brother, Sam, were given a Bar Mitzvah when they were 13 years old.

Even though his parents tried to leave the *shtetl* behind, they taught their children the Jewish ideals from the old country. "Education," "learning," and "study" were words that drove Moe and his brother and sister to excel in their school work. Moe moved ahead from grade to grade getting high marks, except for music—he sang off key.

With a March birthday, Moe was one of the youngest and shortest kids in his class at the South Eighth Street School. When he began kindergarten, then first grade, Moe was swallowed up in a class of close to forty pupils. But whenever he raised his hand to give an answer, his classmates knew that he could be counted on to offer much more information than the teacher expected. Moe always brought home awards and certificates at the end of each school year for attendance, good behavior, attention to study, and good grades.

Although Moe was small, he was not too small to play baseball. No one in the Berg family had ever wanted to throw a ball, much less play baseball, but Moe couldn't remember when he didn't throw a ball or an orange or anything round that could sail through the air. He never tired of the game, throwing a ball back and forth on the dirt street, a narrow alley, anywhere. It was always the same. Catch and throw. Catch and throw. Catch and throw. Sometimes for hours.

Moe joked that he sometimes wondered if he was adopted. Of course he wasn't—he was a true Berg. Still, Moe knew that his father Bernard would watch him catch and throw, then turn away in disgust. Bernard made no secret that he didn't like or understand athletics. Book learning, studying languages—these were worthwhile ways to spend your time.

Moe's mother, Rose, on the other hand, took pleasure in her son's love of baseball. She liked to tell the story of how Moe, when he was almost five, would play catch with their neighbor, Patrolman Hibler. The police officer usually stopped at the Berg's drugstore while walking his beat. Moe would move into the catcher's position behind a manhole cover and pretend he was squatting behind home plate. Officer Hibler would carefully remove his policeman's derby, take off his dark blue, brass buttoned policeman's jacket, and toss the ball.

"Throw harder, Mr. Hibler," Moe would holler.

Then the policeman would pull his arm back and let fly with a hardball, which Moe would catch and shoot right back. Officer Hibler would return the ball faster and harder, but no matter how hard, no matter how fast, Moe caught the ball. His game of catch with the policeman became a neighborhood show. People stopped their pushcarts and horses to watch.

It didn't take long for Moe to figure out that baseball was his ticket to becoming a "real" American—to belonging once and for all. When he played baseball, he felt as if his teammates included him as just another kid. Then no one could single him out as a Jew. All that mattered was that he was a good ballplayer who could bring in a winning score.

Moe's throwing arm brought him respect. It may even have saved him from being roughed up walking to and from school by gangs who didn't like Jews. Besides, his ball playing was making him famous. Newark's Roseville Methodist Episcopal Church baseball team invited him to play with them while he was still in grade school, but not as Moe Berg. His last name didn't fit in with the rest of the team. So, even though Moe wasn't happy with the idea, he played for the Roseville Methodist Episcopal Church as "Runt Wolfe."

Moe couldn't stay away from the game. He was always ready to play with the neighborhood kids. If a player hit a baseball through a window, the whole team earned the money to pay for the damage. Like his teammates, Moe shoveled lots of snow for the neighbors, ran errands, and did what he had to do to help pay for those repairs.

Then his team got a lucky break. The owner of a small farm near the drugstore allowed Moe and the rest of the neighborhood kids to practice baseball there. Moe's team spent hours out on the farm playing and talking about what it would be like to play major league baseball on a real grass diamond. On rainy days they met in basements, porches, anywhere they could, to talk baseball, read the sports pages, and brag about their ball-playing heroes.

Although Moe's father didn't want him to hang out with any baseball team, Moe couldn't hide where he went or what he was doing. The family lived over the drugstore and his father, looking out through the drugstore window, knew every time Moe and his sister and brother left the house or came home.

Moe always tried to please his father, but he knew his father didn't want to understand or take the time to learn the game of baseball. His father could speak many languages, was an educated man and a respected professional, and yet he refused to learn anything about the game his son loved.

Moe always listened to his father's disapproval and anger. It was always the same argument. His father didn't want him playing baseball all the time. And his father certainly didn't want him thinking about it so much.

Moe stood his ground. He would do everything his father wanted him to do in school. He took the college preparatory course, studied Greek and French, and won a medal for his grades in French at Barringer High School. But it wasn't enough. His father grumbled about baseball and put the game down whenever he could.

Despite their quarrels over baseball, Moe admired his father and knew he was a good person. Their neighbors came to Bernard Berg before going to a doctor. If his father could help, he would mix a prescription for them right on the spot. Often he did not charge a poor family for the medicine they needed.

His mother helped in the store, too, sitting behind the cash register until dinner time with a crochet hook and yarn, crocheting pieces so fine they would later be displayed in museums. While her hands were busy, Rose talked to the neighbors. She asked about their families and also made the pharmacy an important part of everyone's life. Moe realized early on that the neighbors tolerated him and his Jewish family because his parents ran the drugstore, which was an important part of the neighborhood, and because he had a good throwing arm.

While Moe was going to high school, the United States was fighting World War I. Even though the war was fought an ocean away in Europe, it was part of everyone's life. The United States needed its citizens to help out, and the Berg family supported the war effort any way it could.

School children like Moe gathered peach pits which were ground up and used to make gas masks. More than 3,500 children enrolled in the Home Gardens Division of the Junior Industrial Army, which worked to ease the food shortage. In the summer of 1917, the Essex County Park Commission converted thirty acres of park land into gardens to be planted and harvested by school students. Some of Moe's high school friends drilled in army-like school units.

By the time he was close to high school graduation Moe was already a celebrity in Newark. Moe never made a throwing error, and sportswriters wrote exciting stories about his "throwing arm." In 1918, they selected him for the "dream team," the best baseball players in Newark's public and private schools.

Even though he held back and seemed shy, Moe loved the way people admired him at the games, and he liked the way girls flirted with him. Most of all, he liked the way it felt to win. But his father would not come to a game to watch him play. Still he knew his father was pleased when his class voted him "Brightest Boy," and when he completed high school in three and a half years. At sixteen, Moe was in the Barringer High School graduating class of 1918.

By mid-September 1918, the end of the war was in sight. At last the Armistice was announced in Newark at 2:45 A.M. on Monday, November 11, 1918. At 5:00 A.M., before the sun was up, the sirens blew. Church bells rang. People screamed for joy, yelled and shouted over the Allied victory. By eight o'clock nothing on wheels moved in Newark. Strangers kissed and hugged in the streets. The victory party went on until dawn the next day. Moe loved that patriotic feeling, the pride that came with being an American.

The end of the war was a time for celebration and a time for planning the future. Moe's college years were ahead. But where did he really fit in? What would he do next?

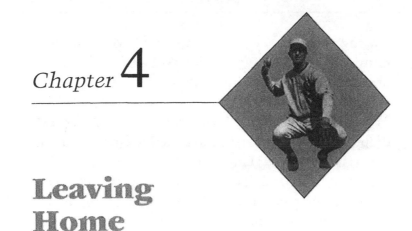

Chapter 4

Leaving Home

Moe's father had always wanted him to become a lawyer. For as long as Moe could remember, his father had warned him never to work for someone else. He told him not to be under the thumb of a boss or someone who could hire or fire him. Bernard had always advised Moe to become a professional. His older brother, Sam, was already doing exactly what their father told him to do, studying at New York University to be a doctor. It was Moe's turn to satisfy his father and mother and make something important of himself, by choosing the law, a worthwhile career.

Moe obediently started classes in September 1918 at New York University in Manhattan, where Sam was already enrolled. The brothers traveled and studied together. Every school morning Moe and Sam climbed on a bus to Newark's Penn Station, ran upstairs and boarded the "Tubes." They sat on straw-colored caned seats, rocking back and forth as the Tubes clacked along over the Jersey Meadows, dropped into the tunnel under the Hudson River, and deposited them in Manhattan.

Sam didn't mind the grind, but after two semesters Moe wanted something different, something better, something that seemed way out of reach: Moe wanted to go to Princeton University. Like his father, he loved foreign languages and wanted to study with the best professors he could find and they were all at Princeton.

This was a new and daring idea for Moe and his family. Princeton did not usually accept students like Moe. He had three strikes against him. He graduated from a public high school, unlike most of Princeton's applicants, who came from exclusive private schools such as Lawrenceville, Choate, Andover, and Newark Academy. His family was poor compared to the rich dynasties who sent their sons to Princeton. He was Jewish at a time when only a few Jews were enrolled at the university. But Moe wanted a "major league" education, and Princeton University was definitely the best.

Moe wanted to believe that he had a fair chance. He wanted to believe that at Princeton, talent and brains were given more respect than wealth or religious background. Just as he did before each baseball game, Moe sized up the situation, then decided on a plan of action. Getting accepted by Princeton University might be tough, but he had a lot going for him. To begin with, he was an excellent student. And just as important to Princeton, he was a great baseball player. Moe figured the university could use a good student who could help them win baseball games.

After filling out the application, Moe had to score high on stiff entrance examinations. He had to prove that his public high school education was just as good as that of the private schools. The day of his Princeton interview Moe got off the Dink, the shuttle train that ran from the main Pennsylvania train line at Princeton Junction to the town of Princeton itself. He walked the few blocks to the university's main iron gates on Nassau Street. Then he presented himself for the examination in languages.

Princeton's classrooms smelled of the well-oiled wood of the worn old walnut desks and chairs, and the musky odor of old stone buildings. Moe sat for his exams and was tested on his ability to translate Homer and Cicero into English, and then on his ability to translate English into Greek and Latin. When the exams were over, he walked along the paths crisscrossing the main campus. Leaving the university behind, he passed the row of stores lining Nassau Street, the student hangout called the "Balt," the town movie theater, historic Whig & Clio Hall, and the Princeton Battle Monument. The small town felt just right to him. Princeton was where he hoped he would belong.

When the letter from the admissions office arrived, it began: "We are pleased to inform you..." His exam grades were between 95 and 100. Moe's parents were overjoyed. In one generation the Berg family had made a giant leap from living in a *shtetl* in the Ukraine to having a son accepted at Princeton University, one of the country's oldest and finest institutions of higher learning. Only in America could this happen.

Moe entered Princeton in the fall of 1919, as part of the class of '23, the first class to enter the university after World War I. At seventeen Moe was one of the youngest among seven hundred freshmen. By the end of their first year, almost half, three hundred, would drop out.

Princeton seemed like another planet to Moe. There was nothing about Princeton that reminded him of the Roseville neighborhood, near Sanford Avenue, with its orphanage, churches, trolleys, and pubs. In his old neighborhood the men came home from factories or work to a bustling street and houses filled with kids. Women were surrounded by noisy children as they cleaned house or carried their bundles of groceries.

Princeton was a small quiet town. From Nassau Street, down to Lake Carnegie on Alexander Road, stood dignified university buildings that resembled European castles or cathedrals set inside a low stone wall. The massive cut stone buildings faced each other on neatly trimmed lawns, shaded by ancient oaks, pines and elms. Few if any children were seen playing outside in the streets.

It was clear to Moe that there were mainly two kinds of students at Princeton: rich and poor. While Moe had just enough money to get by, many of his classmates were wealthy, with fathers who worked as bankers, ambassadors, stockbrokers, manufacturers, or who managed their family's vast fortunes. Their families had been in the United States for generations.

Moe's tuition at Princeton was two hundred dollars a year in 1919. Room and board at the cheapest rooming house cost another four hundred fifty dollars. His costs for a school year came to over six hundred fifty dollars, more than a year's salary for some of his Roseville neighbors.

Moe added to the money his family sent him. At the end of his sophomore year he became a summer counselor at Camp Wah-Kee-Nah in New Hampshire. Of course he also taught baseball there. For most of his Princeton classmates, Christmas holidays meant vacations and parties, or trips south to Florida, but not for Moe. He took the train back to Newark and went to work for the Newark Post Office delivering mail. In his sophomore year he got a scholarship for one hundred twenty-seven dollars, but it just wasn't enough. Eventually, he had to ask for a loan from the university, which he paid back after graduation.

The university was like a big gentlemen's club. All the students knew each other. The undergraduates took for granted that Princeton University was exactly where they belonged and life was exactly as it should be. But once again, Moe was different. Though he didn't show it, he felt he didn't really fit in, just as he hadn't quite belonged at Barringer High School or with his Roseville neighbors. Now at Princeton he was a loner again. In the eyes of his classmates Moe was a Hebrew.

There were few other Jewish students at Princeton. Once again Moe's religion set him apart. Just as at Barringer High, he didn't push his way in where he felt he was not wanted. Most of the time, he was more comfortable not getting too close to anyone. He felt it was easier for everyone that way. Still, Moe

MORRIS BERG. "Bergie," "Mo." He was born in New York City, March 2, 1902, and has also lived in Bristol, N. H.; and Newark, N. J.

He is the son of Bernard Berg and Rose Tasker. His father is a pharmacist. He has one brother and one sister.

Berg prepared at Barringer High School.

In Princeton, he has won General Honors (1) (2) (3); and been a member of the Freshman Baseball Team; Varsity Baseball Team (2) (3) (4); Basketball Squad (2) (3) (4); and Whig Hall.

Freshman year he roomed in 14 North Middle Reunion alone; Sophomore year at 23 William Street with R. P. Sutton '22; Junior year in 6 South West with Sutton; Senior year in 6 South West alone.

He is a Hebrew.

His permanent address is 92 South 13th St., Newark, N. J.

Princeton University graduate, Moe, class of '23. (*Photo courtesy of Princeton University Libraries.*)

wouldn't hide his religion. When a group of Jewish students decided to hold Friday night services on campus, Moe joined them.

Moe loved his classes in French, Spanish, Italian, German, Latin, Greek, and Sanskrit. He also studied the science of language, called linguistics, and spent hours in Princeton's Firestone Library tracking down the history of ancient verbs. When he graduated, it was magna cum laude with a B.A. degree in Languages.

Despite being a loner, Moe still attracted a lot of attention at Princeton. He became known not for his good looks, or his grades, or for all the subjects he was taking, but for the way he could play baseball.

After football, baseball was the second most popular sport on campus. And no one at Princeton was a better baseball player than Moe. When Coach Bill Clarke called for candidates for the baseball team, Moe was accepted as soon as he tried out. He quickly got tagged for the varsity team in the winter of his freshman year.

From the first time he put on the striped uniform of the Orange and Black, Moe felt at home with his teammates and comfortable with them on the baseball diamond. While they all trained together for their games and played against other Ivy League colleges, he felt he belonged, and was a true Princeton man.

Once again, playing baseball earned Moe attention and respect. During his freshman year, he played first base on a team that won every game it played. Sophomore year Moe switched to varsity shortstop, and started every game for the Princeton Tigers from then until he graduated. The strong throwing arm he'd been developing became even better. He had a real feel for the ball and could tell the ball's path just as it left the bat. Even though Moe would never run fast, his baseball sense made up for it. He had a slingshot arm and an ability to hit the ball in the clutch.

Students admired Moe because he was Princeton's number one baseball player. But he was not only a sports star, he also told good jokes and great stories and got excellent grades. Yet Moe felt his classmates shut him out as a close friend because he was different. Still, perhaps because he was a star, the other stu-

Moe (*front row, seated, third from left*) helped Princeton's varsity baseball team win eighteen straight games. (*Photo courtesy of Princeton University Libraries.*)

dents did not close the door completely. In his junior year Moe was invited to join an eating club.

There were no fraternities at Princeton. Instead, the university had eating clubs located in huge homes on Prospect Street. Freshmen and sophomores were required to eat in the university dining halls. But by their junior year, the students were divided into those who belonged to eating clubs and those who had to eat with the lower classmen or at rooming houses.

Each eating club had its own crowd and its own personality—just like any school club. The eating club you belonged to said everything about you. Based on your club membership, people would judge how smart you were, who your parents were, how much money your family had, whether you liked to party a lot, or if you were a great athlete.

Like the rest of his classmates, Moe couldn't ask to join an eating club or choose the one he wanted to belong to. He had to wait for an invitation. The weekend that the eating clubs tapped the students was called Bicker. There was always an air of frantic excitement and tension on campus during Bicker. The students hung around their rooms hoping for a knock on the door from an eating club member with an invitation to join. Everyone understood the invitation was the key to the friends he would have for the rest of his life.

Moe knew he was one of the few Jews at the university to be invited to join an eating club. But the invitation had been offered with an important condition. After Moe became a member, he must agree not to invite any other Jews to join the club. Moe would not agree to that condition. The Friday afternoon of Bicker, he climbed on the Dink to spend the weekend at home in Newark. He knew he had to be on campus to be invited into the club. By leaving campus he showed the eating club what he thought of their invitation and their rule. On Monday when he returned to classes Moe didn't have to explain his actions or his absence from Bicker. No one asked him. It was all understood. For Moe and his classmates, it was easier and more polite this way.

Despite his polite refusal to join an eating club, Moe was popular on campus because he helped win baseball games and brought glory to the Princeton Tigers. Moe had become the star shortstop on one of Coach Bill Clarke's greatest teams. The 1923 varsity team won eighteen games in a row. In his senior year Moe hit .337. In his last game, Moe went out with glory, cracking two hits and batting in Princeton's only home run. Still, Moe had not made a close friend.

As graduation grew near, the seniors voted for outstanding class members. There were forty-one categories from "Best Athlete" to "Most Scholarly." Moe got two votes for "Most Brilliant," but not a single one for "Best Athlete." He wasn't mentioned in any of the other categories.

With his high four-year average and outstanding grades he could have been nominated for the national honor society, Phi Beta Kappa, but he wasn't, and no one ever explained why. He hoped he might be nominated as captain of the baseball team, but he wasn't. Once again, no one explained. Still, someone did recognize that he had done a good job at college. His classics professor, Edmund Robbins, congratulated Moe on both his baseball and scholarship record. But for

Moe, star shortstop on one of Princeton University's all-time greatest baseball teams. (*Photo courtesy of Princeton University Libraries.*)

Moe this was not the same as being told he was one of the best by his classmates.

On graduation day, June 27, Moe faced some hard choices. He had been offered a job at Princeton as an instructor in romance languages. This was a compliment and a reward for his brilliant record, but Moe was ready to move on and he politely turned Princeton down.

His parents had always planned for him to go into law and his father was pushing him to apply to law school. His father wanted to announce proudly that he had a son studying the law. But Moe had his own private plans and secret dreams. He loved playing baseball. It was more than a sport to him. Nothing else mattered as much, not even the education he had just worked so hard to get at Princeton.

Earlier, during his senior year, he had been scouted by two professional baseball teams, the New York Giants and the Brooklyn Robins, later called the Dodgers. Both offered Moe a chance to join their teams as a rookie player. Each team's scouts were eager to have him sign on. They wanted him for a special reason they weren't talking about openly. The pros wanted Moe because he was a Jew. The two National League baseball teams were based in Manhattan and Brooklyn. Both boroughs were filled with large Jewish populations and the franchise owners believed a good Jewish baseball player would attract more Jewish fans. With Moe playing on the team, the owners believed attendance would go up in their ballparks.

Near the end of his senior year both the New York Giants and the Brooklyn Robins offered him more money than he had ever dreamed possible. After graduation he could finally do what he had always wanted to all his life: sign on with a professional baseball team.

While his Princeton classmates were preparing for careers in law, the state department, the stock market and business, Moe was seriously considering two offers for a future in professional baseball.

Meanwhile, his father insisted that Moe do something worthwhile with his life. Bernard flatly refused to hear about a baseball career. He couldn't understand why so many people had nothing to do on a work day but go to a ballfield and watch grown men hit a ball. To him it was a complete waste of time.

Although Moe loved to play baseball, he also loved, respected, and admired his father. It took someone from outside his own world to help Moe make up his mind. Someone who understood how it felt to be pushed by his family to do something, when he wanted to do just the opposite.

While he was agonizing about his future and trying to make up his mind in his senior year, Moe brought his problem to Dutch Carter. From his reputation, Moe knew Dutch had once been the best baseball player at Yale University, much the same way that Moe was Princeton's star player. Dutch had also been scouted by the pros while he pitched his college games and had been offered a contract to play professional baseball after graduating from Yale. Moe knew Dutch was a successful lawyer, just the kind of lawyer that Bernard wanted Moe to be some day, so Moe talked it over with Dutch. Should he play pro baseball and please himself? Or go to law school and please his family? What should he choose?

Dutch explained that his parents had also looked down on professional ballplayers. Like Moe's parents, they hadn't wanted him to sign a contract to play ball. Dutch told Moe he had always been sorry that he listened to his family and advised Moe to give baseball a try. Moe understood all too well. Dutch Carter was a famous, successful lawyer, but he had never had a chance to find out if he had what it takes to make it as a major league baseball player.

Dutch's story was just what Moe needed to help him make up his mind. The lawyer convinced Moe to follow his dream and give himself the chance that comes only once in a lifetime. Moe decided not to go to law school, at least not yet. Despite his father's angry objections, Moe turned to the majors. He decided that after graduation from Princeton, he would play baseball for Brooklyn.

Moe was a practical man. The baseball season lasted only a few months out of the year. The rest of the time he would follow his other dream—to be a scholar and a man of learning. With the money he would earn playing pro baseball, he could support his other love, the study of languages. More than anything he wanted to travel to France where he could speak and study the language he knew only through textbooks. He could attend the famous university, the Sorbonne, where he would learn the science of language called experimental phonetics, and study with its founder, the respected scholar, L'Abbé Jean-Pierre Rousselot. When he signed the contract, the Dodgers handed him a check for five thousand dollars. At last he could go to Paris.

Princeton University had helped Moe leave Newark far behind. It had offered new ideas and wonderful

After graduating from Princeton in 1923, Moe signed a contract with the Brooklyn Dodgers. *(Photo courtesy of Princeton University Libraries.)*

possibilities. Most of all it had opened the door to a fresh start on an exciting career.

Moe's lifestyle, which combined sports and scholarly research, seemed unusual to everyone, especially the sportswriters. But not to Moe. He had it all figured out.

Chapter 5

Rookie Moe

In the summer of 1923, Moe started his new life. On June 28, he put on the blue and white colors of the Brooklyn Robins, the team that Brooklyn baseball fans would soon nickname the Brooklyn Dodgers.

Joining his new teammates, Moe boarded a train at Penn Station in New York. They were headed for Philadelphia, where the Brooklyn team was scheduled to play the Phillies in an afternoon game at the Baker Bowl.

After suiting up, Moe sat impatiently in the visitor's dugout. His Princeton coach, Bill Clarke, and some friends clapped and cheered from the bleachers as he came up to bat for the first time. Clarke had been the one to tell the Brooklyn coach about Moe. Now, both men watched to see how Moe's first game would turn out.

By the seventh inning Brooklyn was ahead 13—4. With a safe lead, the Robins' manager decided to give Moe his first big chance. Moe tried to look calm as he entered the game. Bobbing and scooting at shortstop, Moe didn't let his team down. In the ninth inning he converted Cy Williams' line drive into a double play that ended the game. He hadn't done as well at bat, but he managed to bounce a single to drive in a run against Philadelphia.

Brooklyn took the first game of the season series, 15—5. After the game, Moe was surrounded by newspaper reporters who understood that the rookie was a sensational news story. At a time when some players barely finished grade school and many never made it through high school, Moe was an unusually well-educated player. With Moe, the sportswriters had a dazzling new combination to write about. They could tell their readers about Moe Berg, the Princeton graduate who was a rookie shortstop. As for Moe, he enjoyed trading jokes and one-liners with the reporters. He liked being a celebrity. More than anything, he liked being liked and knowing that he belonged.

But Moe played only a few games in July. He felt as if he was getting splinters from sitting on the bench. Then, as the hot summer wore on and Brooklyn dropped further and further back in the National League, the manager let him play more games. By September he was starting regularly. When the season ended, he had appeared in forty-nine games, made twenty-two errors and batted .186. Mike Gonzales, a major league scout summed up Moe's ability in a report he wired to his home office. He sent a four word message: "Good field, no hit." Moe was to carry that label for the rest of his career.

But his mother thought Moe was the greatest baseball player ever. Rose was his number-one fan and proudly bragged to all the customers in the drugstore about her son. She organized relatives and friends for a trip to the ballpark whenever the Dodgers played in Brooklyn. When Moe played, his quiet mother yelled, screamed, and cheered him from the stands. His father, on the other hand, refused to come to the ballpark to watch him play ball. Bernard was furious, believing that Moe was wasting his time. Baseball was a child's game. He did not want Moe to play baseball at all.

That summer, the Dodgers carefully watched Moe to see if he had it in him to be a great ballplayer. For his part, Moe was also finding out whether he really wanted the life of a pro ballplayer. At the very least, playing baseball over the summer would give him the money to pay off his college loan. It would also provide him with money for the trip to Paris and tuition at the Sorbonne.

Finally, the long hot summer was over. He had saved all his paychecks, and he was ready to leave for France. Arriving in Paris, Moe enrolled in the Sorbonne. He stepped out of baseball into a different world, a life that had nothing to do with baseball or sports. He was back to being a student.

In the same way his father and grandfather had studied for the love of learning, Moe studied the romance languages, asking questions, considering possibilities, and examining hidden meanings. Moe searched for knowledge throughout that cold Paris winter. He was a scholar, a searcher, a student, and life was good.

For the next six months, Moe and Professor L'Abbé Rousselot studied linguistics, the science of language. Together they traced the history of the ancient Latin languages and how each mixed with the other. The pair worked mostly with the romance languages, including Romanian, Italian, French, Spanish, and Portuguese.

Living in Paris was wonderful. Moe loved the lively city despite its bad winter weather. On cold nights, he shut the windows against the rain, and he watched the wind strip the leaves from the trees. He found good wood for sale, and learned to keep warm with "boulets," molded egg-shaped lumps of coal, on the wood fire. Moe heard of other Americans who were hanging out together in Paris, writers named Ernest Hemingway, Gertrude Stein, and Zelda and F. Scott Fitzgerald, but Moe wasn't interested in making friends. His studies, his books, and his newspapers kept him busy. He searched for what he wanted on the printed page—that was all the company he needed.

The off-season months passed too soon. Slowly the grayness of Paris changed. The naked trees began to bud. Icy cobblestone streets began to ooze mud. The sun was brighter, the days longer. The long winter finally came to an end. Spring training for 1924 was starting. It was time to return to baseball. Moe's other life was waiting for him across the Atlantic Ocean, in Brooklyn.

When he reported to the Dodgers Moe discovered they had traded him. He had been optioned to a minor league franchise, Minneapolis, for the first half of the season, then traded to Toledo for the rest of the year. Although he hated the minors, Moe wouldn't quit. He knew he wasn't a great player for either club, batting .264 with a one hundred ten hit season. By 1925, Moe was traded again, this time to the Reading Keys of the International League, a minor league team out of Reading, Pennsylvania. With its farms and pretzel factories, Reading was worlds away from the streets of Paris and France.

Moe told friends that if he couldn't get back into the majors, he would get out of baseball and maybe try to return to Princeton and teach. Moe always believed that if you couldn't do it well, you shouldn't do it at all. He gave Reading his best shot, and it worked. He batted .311, drove in one hundred twenty-four runs, collected two hundred hits, and hit nine home runs.

Once again, sportswriters were telling their readers about Moe Berg, comparing him to the best players in the majors. This new commotion about his career was just what Moe was hoping for. He was a headline maker and a baseball star all over again, and it felt just great. He had worked hard at shortstop, batted over .340 that summer and now the majors wanted him back.

Two top teams, the Chicago White Sox and the New York Yankees, bid for him. In November the White Sox won out. Earlier that season they had offered Reading $6,000 for his contract. Reading said no. Thanks to Moe's excellent performance throughout the season, the White Sox tried again. It made headlines when Charles Comiskey paid Reading $50,000 for the rights to Moe Berg. This was a huge amount of money in 1925, when a hot dog cost a nickel, a bottle of milk was twelve cents, a newspaper sold for three cents, and a family could live well on a thousand dollars a year.

In 1925, Moe was traded to the Chicago White Sox for $50,000. *(Photo courtesy of National Baseball Library and Archives, Cooperstown, NY.)*

To Moe's father, baseball was not a "real" profession, no matter how much people paid. He kept urging Moe to think about his life after baseball. His brother Sam was a doctor. His sister Ethel was a kindergarten teacher. Shouldn't Moe become a professional, too? Didn't he want to study the law? Once again his father insisted that Moe choose between baseball and the law. This time, to satisfy his father, Moe finally agreed to go to law school.

He applied to Columbia University Law School in New York City without mentioning his career as a baseball player or that he was living far away in Chicago. After Columbia accepted him, Moe figured out how to juggle his full-time baseball career with his full-time law school schedule. He would go to Columbia law school in the off-season and use the money from playing baseball to pay for his law school tuition.

At first, when Moe didn't show up for spring training in 1926, Charles Comiskey, the coaches, and Moe's teammates didn't object. Moe told them he would join the club in six weeks, when law school was over. When he finally appeared, the White Sox were starting another shortstop, rookie Bill "Honey Boy" Hunnefield. The White Sox finished fifth that season. In forty-one games Moe hit only .221. The White Sox used Hunnefield regularly, while Moe warmed the bench.

That winter Charles Comiskey, fed up with his team's poor play, decided he had had enough of Moe's schedule. Comiskey had paid for Moe's contract. He owned Moe's time as a baseball player. The White Sox owner didn't want his shortstop to even think about skipping spring training. He ordered Moe to report along with all the other team members. Moe was going to have to obey the rules just like everyone else or leave the game. If he wanted time off to go to law school, he had to forget pro baseball. The owner spelled it all out in a letter to Moe, telling him he had to choose between baseball and a career in law.

Moe read Comiskey's letter and realized he was at a crossroads. Baseball was in his blood and in his heart. On the other hand, he knew he had to think of a future career because he couldn't play baseball forever. Upset, Moe didn't know which way to turn. While he was thinking it over, Moe continued going to classes at Columbia.

One day he stopped in to ask Professor Noel Dowling about a lesson in law. As he entered Dowling's office, Moe saw his professor reading the sports pages. Putting down the paper, Dowling mentioned that the Giants had beaten Pittsburgh. It was clear that Dowling had no idea Moe was a professional baseball player. He added that he had played first base for Vanderbilt University. Moe told him he had played for Princeton.

Suddenly the professor realized who Moe was and Moe told him about the terrible choice he was being forced to make. Then Moe asked Dowling for a favor. If baseball would not change its spring training schedule, could Columbia University change its course schedule?

Professor Dowling went over Moe's courses. He figured out a schedule for the spring term that would give Moe a leave of absence from Columbia University. After the baseball season was over, Moe could return to classes at the law school. By taking twice as many courses in the off-season, Moe would be free for the White Sox and spring training.

Once again Moe was part of two different worlds. When he wasn't playing baseball, he studied law. As much as he could he continued to pursue his passion for linguistics, which he had studied in Paris.

But for all the work it took to stay with the White Sox, the 1927 season turned out to be a big disappointment. Moe played in only thirty-five games, hitting .246. The only real action came from reporters hunting for a sports story. They liked Moe, and he liked them. Reporters got into the habit of following Moe around and making everything he did appear important in their newspapers. From then on, Moe would always be big news.

Meanwhile, Charles Comiskey kept Moe behind Honey Boy as shortstop for most of that summer. Finally, in late August, Moe got his big break. In a series against Philadelphia, Ray Schalk, the Sox' manager-catcher, broke his hand when a batter swung and hit it. Backup catcher Buck Crouse ripped his finger open on a foul tip. Then, third-string catcher Harry McCurdy fractured his finger.

Ray Schalk frantically yelled to his road secretary, "Get us a catcher. Quick!"

Still warming the bench, Moe calmly called out, "What do you mean get a catcher? You've got a catcher sitting on this bench." Although he hadn't said so, Moe meant Earl Sheely, who had caught in the minors. Schalk, thinking that Moe was talking about himself, told Moe to get outfitted.

While the fans watched, hooted, hollered, whistled and yelled, Moe put on the "tools of ignorance" as the catcher's equipment was called, tested different catcher's mitts until he found one he liked, walked out on the diamond, and took some throws at home plate. The game was suspended as players, umpires,

Wearing the tools of ignorance, Moe discovered his natural position as a catcher. (*Photo courtesy of National Baseball Library and Archives, Cooperstown, NY.*)

and thousands of fans watched to see what would happen next.

His first throw to second base got wedged between the bag and the ground. Whistles and catcalls came from the stands. Moe ignored them. Then he settled in and played the game. Moe had never caught in the majors before, but he made no errors at his new position.

The White Sox won 4–1. But it was an even bigger victory for Moe. He knew he had finally found his natural position. He was a defensive catcher.

Chapter 6

First-String Catcher

Moe liked kneeling behind the plate, calling the pitches. It was the first time he had played catcher since he was a school kid in Newark. To him the catcher's signals were like another language, and he learned them as quickly as he had mastered so many other languages.

The real test for Moe would be Chicago's next game in New York against the world champion Yankees. Chicago's ace, Ted Lyons, was scheduled to pitch. The White Sox could use one of their three injured catchers or they could use Moe. Ted Lyons quickly settled the question. The White Sox ace asked for Berg behind the plate. He felt sure the new catcher could do the job.

When the great Babe Ruth came up to bat, Moe was catching. If he was nervous, he didn't show it. Years later sportswriters would tell how the Babe joked, "Moe, you're going to be the fourth wounded White Sox catcher by the fifth inning."

"That's all right," Moe shot back. "I'll only call for inside pitches and we'll keep each other company in the hospital." Both laughed. Then Ted Lyons struck out the great Babe Ruth.

Moe caught in nine more games that year. He had good reactions, a strong arm, and great hands. He studied the batters, learning their weaknesses and

White Sox catcher Moe helped pitchers feel confident.
(*Photo courtesy of National Baseball Library and Archives, Cooperstown, NY.*)

their strengths, and used what he learned to call the signals. Pitchers felt more confident when Moe was catching. His shortstop experience helped him behind the plate, as he easily picked up the short hops that most catchers would miss.

Still, Moe was struggling at bat. He knew he needed more batting practice. After the games Moe would follow pitchers into the showers and beg them to work out with him at dawn in Comiskey Park. Not wanting more work and needing their sleep, the pitchers tried to avoid Moe. They couldn't understand Moe or his different ways. But because he was so eager and excited about the game they struggled out of bed and came with him. And slowly he improved his batting average.

During his years with the White Sox, Moe began reading foreign newspapers—a practice he would continue throughout his life. Just as his teammates read the Chicago papers, Moe read French, Italian, and German newspapers. He would buy them on his way to the ballpark, carefully fold them up and put them into neat piles. If anyone touched or handled his fresh newspapers before he finished reading them, Moe lost his temper, threw them out, and bought new ones.

By the 1928 season, Moe was sharing catching duties with Crouse, McCurdy, and Schalk. He played seventy-three games that year, and unlike many other players, he never once argued with or fought against the umpires. Moe understood that he could get more by using his head than by using his fists on the diamond. In a soft, deep voice, Moe would kid with the umpires to correct a bad call. Moe usually wouldn't back down, but with a laugh or with a joke he would get the umpires to see the play and the game his way.

Moe used his head to distract the players up at bat, too. From behind his catcher's mask he'd ask a "friendly question" about the batter's family, or his parents, or something else. It was just enough to take the batter's mind off the ball hurtling toward him. Just enough to change the rhythm of the batter's swing. And just enough, sometimes, to make the player strike out.

During the off-season, Moe returned to law school. His mother and father were pleased that he was going to have a "real" profession. At last Moe was listening to their advice and would have a career that mattered.

For Moe, 1929 was a great year. The early dawn practice had paid off and he was hitting his stride. His batting average improved to .287 and he made only seven errors all season, leading American League catchers in fielding. Once again he was the hot ballplayer sportswriters wanted to write about and readers wanted to read about. Twenty-five American League players received votes for the Most Valuable Player award that year. Moe received two votes, a great honor. Bill Dickey of the Yankees, the only other catcher nominated, got six votes. Al Simmons of Philadelphia won the MVP. Still, Moe was pleased to have made the list at all.

Fame brought constant invitations to parties and Moe soon learned to bring his black dinner jacket to the locker room for a quick change. He never worried about dinner any more because he could always be sure of an invitation and a party.

Though he often had dates, Moe wasn't involved with just one girlfriend. He loved taking attractive women to night clubs and restaurants and ordering the best and most expensive wines and food. He was tall and broad shouldered, and most women reached up only as far as his shoulders. His size and his attentiveness made women feel special. Moe tried to find something interesting to talk about: the news, politics, baseball, whatever his date wanted to discuss. He could easily hold a conversation in many languages, not just English. Still, Moe always made sure not to get too close or too involved with anyone.

This was Moe's way. At a party he could be telling stories and jokes one minute and then vanish without a word or good-bye the next. He liked his freedom and didn't want to share his life or explain himself to anyone. He wanted to be able to travel, with no one waiting for him or asking questions.

In the off-season, Moe went to classes, did his homework, and worked hard at law school. In February 1930, he got his law degree. Soon afterwards, he was on his way to the White Sox spring training in San Antonio, Texas. Moe was primed for the season. That same year, he became the White Sox' starting catcher—in the same month that he passed the tough New York State Bar exam, the exam every law school graduate had to pass in order to practice law in New York State.

When spring training ended Moe headed north with the other White Sox players. Because good catchers were hard to find, other American League clubs now wanted him, but Moe turned down their offers out of loyalty to the White Sox. A week before the season's opening game in Chicago, Moe and his team were playing in an exhibition game at Little Rock, Arkansas. It was an unimportant game to the White

Sox, but it turned out to be an important game for Moe.

Hustling off first base, Moe started to steal second. Realizing he couldn't make it, he turned back, trying to beat the pick-off throw. As he changed direction, his spikes caught in the dirt. Suddenly, his right leg twisted under him. In terrible pain, he barely crawled back to first base. The ligaments in his right knee were badly ruptured and Moe was rushed to Chicago's Mercy Hospital for knee surgery. Meanwhile the club announced that it was only a minor injury and Moe would return to the lineup in a month.

To speed up his recovery after the surgery, Moe's knee was treated daily with heat in a special "baking machine," but Moe knew better than anyone that the heat, the help from the doctors, and the exercise with the physical therapists weren't enough. His right leg would never be the same again. He had never been a fast base runner, and now he would be even slower. After leaving the hospital, he had more bad luck, contracting bronchial pneumonia.

As he recovered, he realized how very much he missed the game. Pushing and punishing himself, he worked to get into shape for the rest of the baseball season. Moe understood that he ought to leave baseball for good and become a full-time lawyer. He could walk away from baseball without any excuses or apologies. Everyone would understand why he had quit the game. But he couldn't make himself do it. He had to give himself one more chance, to play just one more season.

After the season ended, he took a job in the Manhattan law firm of Satterlee and Canfield. He was hired because he knew many foreign languages and could handle foreign clients and law contracts. It was a good fit because his bosses knew he was a part-time lawyer who wanted to work only in baseball's off-season.

After being traded to Cleveland, Moe slowly changed from player to coach. *(Photo courtesy of National Baseball Library and Archives, Cooperstown, NY.)*

For Moe, 1930 had been an awful year. He had played only twenty games for the White Sox. By the time the season rolled around in 1931, the White Sox were convinced that Moe's major league days were over. Still, he wouldn't give in or agree. He didn't want to become a full-time lawyer, and sit at a desk in an office, following the same routine day after day. He tried to push himself back into the lineup, but he sat out most of the games, playing only twenty games that summer and batting .115.

In April 1931, the White Sox sold him to the Cleveland Indians, but the Cleveland team already had three great catchers, Luke Swell, Glynn Matt, and Joe Spring. Moe was back on the bench, sometimes going for weeks without a chance to put on his catcher's mask and get into the game. Moe played only ten games for Cleveland that season. Slowly, he began to change from player to coach. New recruits, the young pitchers and catchers who joined the team, were coming to him for baseball advice. They stayed to hear his ideas and adventures.

At the end of January 1932, the Indians gave Moe his unconditional release. That March, he was invited to the Washington Senators spring training camp.

Moe didn't play in many games that year. Instead he warmed up players, yelled advice to pitchers, hollered encouragement to his team. Did it bother Moe not to play often? Whatever he felt deep down, Moe didn't complain, even when the Giants defeated the Senators four games to one in the World Series.

Outside the ballparks, the United States was suffering through the Great Depression. People were losing jobs. Men, women, and children went hungry and lived on the streets because they had nowhere else to go. Moe heard that some of his Princeton classmates had lost their fortunes and were working for hand-outs. Some even came to Moe for loans. With two paychecks, one from baseball, and another from the law office, Moe didn't have money troubles.

Moe hit .246 for the Washington Senators in 1932 and caught seventy-five games. *(Photo courtesy of AP/Wide World Photos.)*

His older brother, Dr. Sam, understood that Moe was well off. Sam tried to convince their father that Moe was earning a lot of money and he was doing better than many of his Princeton classmates, but Bernard refused to listen. He would not change his mind about Moe's playing baseball.

By the end of the 1932 season, Moe had played for the Washington team more than he thought he would. He caught seventy-five games, hitting .246 for the season and coming through with several game-winning clutch hits for the Senators. In May, the Senators manager put him back behind the plate to catch in a series against the White Sox.

Moe faced his ex-teammate Ted Lyons one hot afternoon. The two players liked and respected each other, but each wanted to win. Ted Lyons was still on the mound in the fourteenth inning with the score tied at 5–5 when Moe had a key hit to win the game.

The game over, Moe ran to the Senators' dugout with Ted Lyons chasing him. Moe was doubled up with laughter. Ted got to Moe in the locker room and gave him a couple of friendly jabs. The story goes that Ted joked, "Why'd you have to pick on me? You haven't had a hit in twenty years!" Still doubled over, Moe was laughing too hard to answer—he could only shake his head. It was a great way to close the season.

Chapter 7

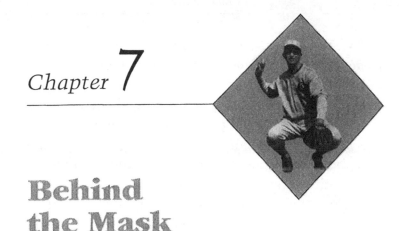

Behind the Mask

In October of 1932, Moe was hired to go to Japan with Ted Lyons and Dodger outfielder Lefty O'Doul. The Japanese were crazy about baseball. An American sports agent was putting together teams of American baseball stars to travel to Japan to put on exhibitions and to teach the game. Moe and the others became part of the tour. Moe studied the Japanese language before the trip and worked on it as the trio traveled halfway around the world. By the time they arrived, he had learned enough to speak some Japanese, which pleased and astonished their hosts.

The three players traveled to six Japanese universities where they gave classes in pitching, catching, and batting. At the end of their Japanese tour, they went in different directions. Moe's teammates headed back to the States, but Moe wanted to keep traveling. From Japan, he went to Korea and China. Then he went to India to study with Sanskrit masters. Years later people would wonder if Moe had a special secret reason for taking this unusual trip halfway around the world. Was he using baseball as a cover to gather information about countries that few Americans visited?

With the languages, sounds, sights, and politics of half the world still swimming in his head, Moe reached Berlin, Germany, by the end of January 1933, shortly after Adolf Hitler was appointed Chancellor of the Reichstag.

Moe saw that Hitler was taking over Germany. The Germans were marching in uniforms, goose-stepping with outstretched arms, and chanting war songs. Sensing trouble, Moe quickly returned to New York. Moe realized that Adolf Hitler and Germany were going to turn the world into a battlefield. Though only a few of his friends wanted to listen or believe his predictions, Moe was certain he was right.

During the 1933 season, Moe became more secretive than ever about his life away from the baseball park. Returning to the Senators' locker room after a game, Moe usually reached for his dinner jacket or black tails and white tie. Handsome, over six feet tall, with glistening dark black wavy hair and a lean athlete's build, he always had an invitation to a foreign embassy dinner or party. His reputation as a scholar, his clever stories, and his Princeton diploma had opened doors in the nation's capitol that were tightly closed to other famous baseball players. At home on the baseball diamond, Moe was equally at home in the Washington world of foreign embassies, formal state dinners, and parties filled with government officials. It was also a world of undercover agents, secret couriers, sealed reports, and spies.

At the parties, Moe shook hands with the growing list of diplomats, politicians, and statesmen he called friends. He kissed the hands of pretty women in long beautiful party gowns and complimented them in their native languages. As the orchestra played, he picked the prettiest single woman and whirled her across the dance floor. Moe looked as if he was just there to have a good time, but he always seemed to have a secret reason for attending all those parties.

By the end of July 1934, Moe was finished with the Senators. The team was losing more games than it was winning. Benched for most of the season, Moe hadn't been much help to the team.

What would he do next? The reporters demanded he tell them.

As it turned out, Moe's contract was quickly picked up by Cleveland and Moe finished out that season as the Indians' reserve catcher. That year, Moe set a new American League record for catching in 117 consecutive games (from 1931 to 1934 for Chicago, Washington, and Cleveland) without making an error.

In the late fall of 1934, an all-star team that included Babe Ruth, Connie Mack, Lou Gehrig, Lefty Gomez, and Charlie Gehringer was getting ready to tour Japan. Connie Mack invited Moe to come along as an interpreter, coach, and player. On October 20, Moe and the other players and their wives boarded a ship in Vancouver, Canada. When they arrived in Tokyo, the Japanese crowds greeted them cheering and waving. The Japanese were eager to see the tall, strong, easygoing, gum-chewing, tobacco-spitting American baseball stars.

Moe had been invited to give a speech at Meiji University. Facing Japanese students who were eager to see an American baseball player, he began to speak, amazing his audience by giving his speech in fluent Japanese.

Though he wasn't on the diamond much, Moe was having the time of his life. He posed with geishas, attended parties and dinners in honor of the American

On the Japanese tour, interpreter, coach, and player Moe talked baseball with all-star pitcher Lefty O'Doul and Sotaro Suzuki of the Tokyo Baseball Club. *(Photo courtesy of National Baseball Library and Archives, Cooperstown, NY.)*

baseball players, and served as the team's interpreter, coach, and goodwill ambassador. He had brought along a movie camera and took movies like any other tourist.

But this was a front for a secret mission that had come from the office of the President of the United States. Moe was actually carrying a letter from the U.S. Secretary of State, Cordell Hull, introducing him to several Japanese diplomats so that he would be invited to their receptions and to some meetings. Acting on a special set of secret instructions from his government, Moe was to listen, watch, and later report to Washington on everything he saw and heard in Japan.

Quietly, he followed his orders and soaked up information for the United States. While he smiled and talked baseball, he used his photographic memory and movie camera to record information to take back home. When the other ballplayers and their wives toured the sights in Japan, Moe went off somewhere else, always by himself. His teammates joked that he was always moving about, always coming from some place or other, but he never offered to explain where he'd been. Finally they stopped asking him.

One day he didn't show up at the Tokyo ballpark for an exhibition game. No one on the team knew where he was. Even though Moe wasn't scheduled to catch that day, he was expected to be in uniform and in the bullpen, ready to warm up pitchers or to play, if necessary. The game went on without Moe. Later, when his teammates caught up with him, Moe insisted he missed the game because he didn't feel well. But his answer didn't satisfy the other players. They knew Moe didn't get sick often. Besides, he hadn't told his friend

Babe Ruth or reported to Manager Connie Mack that he was sick. Though they grumbled, the team put Moe's unexplained absence aside. They were having too good a time in Japan to let him spoil it.

While his teammates were on the ballfield, Moe had walked across Tokyo to St. Luke's Hospital, one of the tallest buildings in the city. St. Luke's was seven floors tall, a skyscraper by Tokyo standards. Carrying a bouquet of fresh flowers Moe had smiled and bowed to the guard in the reception area. He announced that he was visiting the American ambassador's daughter, who had given birth to a baby girl. The guard waved Moe on to the elevator. Still smiling and bowing Moe entered the elevator and pushed the button for the top floor, where he got out and climbed to the roof of the hospital. A perfect view of the city of Tokyo lay before him.

Taking his movie camera from its hiding place underneath his coat, Moe shot footage of the city. He took pictures of important buildings, oil refineries, the layout of the center of Tokyo, the factories, and the shipyards. He worked quickly, hoping that he wouldn't be discovered. Satisfied that he'd gotten what he came for, Moe hastily left the roof and climbed back down to the top floor. He rang for the elevator and took it to the ground floor, returning the bow of the Japanese guard who wished him good-bye. Then he walked out of the hospital, back to the ballfield and his buddies. He never saw the ambassador's daughter.

Eight years later during World War II, General Jimmy Doolittle led sixteen B-25 bombers on a raid of Tokyo. Those American bombers were the first to carry the war back to the enemy's doorstep. The photos the

U. S. military used to identify the target buildings for that raid included pictures that Moe had taken years earlier from the roof of St. Luke's Hospital.

Chapter **8**

Tourist or Spy?

After the baseball all-star tour of Japan ended and their Japanese hosts had given them parties, taken lots of pictures, and promised them everlasting friendship, Babe Ruth, Casey Stengel, and the other players and their wives returned to the United States.

Moe had other plans, however. He was going back home by a different route, a route that would take him on the mysterious Trans-Siberian Railroad. This trip involved a six-day journey from Manchuria through Siberia in temperatures of 35 degrees below zero. The railroad, built in 1899 by the Russians to move raw timber to western markets, starts in Manchuria and ends more than 4,000 miles later in Moscow.

Moe remained in Japan for two weeks after the others had left. Then he boarded the *Empress of Canada* for Shanghai, spent one day at the Hotel Grand, and then flew to Peking where he toured the city for four days. On New Year's Eve, 1934, Moe boarded the Trans-Siberian Railroad to ride it all the way to Moscow, one of the few Americans to take that long trip. If the other passengers were curious about the American, then the American seemed just as curious about them and their countries.

No one feared or suspected an American baseball player on a holiday. Especially a baseball player who was polite and easy to talk to and who tried to speak the languages of his traveling companions as he cheerfully snapped endless pictures from the windows of the swaying railroad cars while the train slowly puffed its way from Asia to Russia.

Moe's journey took him through thousands of miles of a gigantic frontier cut off from the outside world. Only a very few people in the United States knew about that dreary but powerful country. Some parts were treeless, with sixty-mile-an-hour winds in the summer and gales that brought snowdrifts fifty feet high in the winter. Sometimes the bare landscape was interrupted by the camps of slave laborers, prisoners who worked in the forests, salt mines, and gold fields. Moe was traveling through a bleak and vast land that was just beginning to develop. Important hydroelectric projects were starting up and there were rich deposits of rare minerals and much-needed ores.

Rocking back and forth in the train, trying to keep warm, Moe traveled across snow-capped mountains eastward through frozen forests and snow-covered plains. Now and again the train stopped and a few

64

Moe had a low batting average, but he had a good arm and could still catch. *(Photo courtesy of AP/Wide World Photos.)*

passengers stepped off and disappeared into an icy no man's land. All the while Moe continued to snap photos as the train jolted and bumped its way toward Russia. Arriving in Moscow on January 6, 1935, Moe swung off the train and stretched his legs. He had crossed from Asia to Europe, taking photos all the way. He was glad to leave the bleak, frozen winter in Moscow and head home.

No one questioned why Moe had taken this unusual trip or why he had taken so many photos. Was there another reason for his journey? Was there a secret reason that he could not talk about? Did he have orders from a government official in Washington to get information on a part of the world so remote from the United States? Even years later, the question of why he took this strange trip would go unanswered.

When Moe returned to the United States, he found a warm welcome. While he had been away, his baseball buddy, Joe Cronin, had joined the Red Sox. Cronin was now the Red Sox manager, with absolute power over his team. One of Cronin's first decisions was, "Bring back Moe Berg. If he can be found..." When Moe arrived in Boston he had a job as a player-coach waiting for him if he wanted it. Moe wanted it. He was a free agent and needed a job in baseball. He wasn't working for Satterlee and Canfield any longer because being an attorney just didn't interest him. The offer from Cronin was the perfect answer.

At thirty-three, Moe knew he was an old man for baseball. This was his fifth team. Even so, Moe would play for Cronin for five more years. Though he had a low batting average, Moe still had a good arm and he could still catch. Lefty Grove and Jack Wilson, Boston Red Sox pitchers, asked for Moe to catch, much the same way the White Sox players had asked for him years earlier. But more and more Moe would come to a practice session, sit in the dugout and talk baseball rather than play the game. Moe liked to be part of the baseball scene and to hang out with the players, and he was satisfied.

One of his favorite new friends was a young Red Sox bat boy named John Fitzgerald Kennedy. Their easygoing jokes and talks didn't end at Fenway Park. Years later when John Fitzgerald Kennedy became president of the United States, Moe would be invited to the White House to talk about baseball and the days at Fenway.

As the years went by, Moe would do more and more unusual things with no explanations. If he seemed odd, people just shrugged it off. Two years after his trip to Japan, Moe startled everyone with his strange behavior before the 1935 pennant game at Yankee Stadium.

The Yankees had been warming up on the field before the game. Moe was in the visitors' dugout with the rest of the Red Sox team, pacing up and down, waiting for their turn on the field. Out on the diamond, Lou Gehrig was at first base, catcher Bill Dickey stood at home plate and Joe DiMaggio and Jake Dosell were catching fly balls in the outfield. The two teams would meet only when the game began.

Suddenly, a lone Red Sox player moved away from the cluster of other uniformed players in the Red Sox dugout. He walked past the players throwing and scooping up balls. He moved slowly across the outfield toward the Yankee bullpen where Lefty Gomez was warming up. That lone Red Sox, Moe Berg, headed straight for Lefty, who had just finished throwing.

Lefty was astonished to see Moe. Over the years, Lefty would tell what happened, why Moe took that unusual walk in front of thousands of curious fans. There, on the diamond, right before the big game, Moe wanted to talk about the trip to Japan they'd both taken two years earlier. Moe was particularly interested in the pictures Lefty had taken of Yokohama Harbor, Shanghai, and Hong Kong with his 16mm camera, which could film from a distance.

While the whistles and catcalls of the impatient baseball fans grew louder, Moe calmly questioned Lefty about those pictures of Japan. Then Moe asked Lefty to send his pictures to Washington, promising that they would be sent back to him. Satisfied that Lefty would do as he was asked, Moe returned to the Red Sox dugout, and the game began.

True to his word, Lefty sent his films to the address Moe had given him. Six months later the films reappeared at Lefty's home with a letter from Washington thanking him for the films, but offering no explanation. Lefty was puzzled but not surprised. It seemed like just another one of Moe's odd, unexplained arrangements. Was Moe working as a secret American agent at that time? To this day, no one knows for sure.

On a cold February night in New York in 1938, Moe faced a microphone at the National Broadcasting Company. He was appearing as a contestant on one of radio's most popular quiz shows, a weekly program called *Information Please*. The baseball owners had asked Moe to appear on *Information Please* to prove to the world that baseball players were smart and classy.

In the days before TV, millions of Americans listened to their radios for hours every day, seven days a week. Every week on *Information Please* guests appeared and a host asked them questions. The guest who answered correctly won prizes. Standing before the microphone in his well-cut business suit, Moe looked like a dignified banker, lawyer, or college professor. Without missing a beat, Moe shot back his answers to each question.

"Venus is the brightest star we see."

"Poi is the Hawaiian substitute for bread."

"A letter called the Boreau Letter was the evidence that convicted an innocent Frenchman, Captain Alfred Dreyfus, of being a spy...."

Every answer was right on the mark. Overnight, Moe became as famous as any well-known movie star. Moe had shown the world that a baseball player could hold his own against the experts who made up quiz shows.

The producers urged Moe to come back to the show and try again. For this next time, a group of newspaper reporters made up a list of test questions. All America was listening to the program that night. The show's host, John Kiernan, a sportswriter for the New York Times, asked Moe the questions. Could an athlete, a baseball player, outwit, outsmart and outthink the best reporters in the newspaper business?

Soon everyone realized that the reporters had used the number seven for all their questions. "Who or what are the Seven Sleepers, the Seven Wise Masters, the Seven Wise Men, the Seven Wonders of the World, and the Seven Stars?"

Every answer Moe gave on the quiz show was correct. Once again he had a perfect 100 percent, and once again he was a sensation. Moe became more famous than most movie stars. In fact, he was as well known as the first full-length Walt Disney cartoon movie, *Snow White and the Seven Dwarfs*, which had just come out.

Moe began to see his name in the news section instead of just on the sports pages of newspapers. Reporters followed him everywhere. For weeks after the show Moe pushed past fans from all across the country who were shoving newspapers at him to autograph. Months later, at the beginning of the baseball season in April, the fans still hadn't let up. After opening day thousands of letters arrived at Fenway Park. Boxes stuffed with letters kept coming all through the season. But Moe wouldn't open any of the letters. Not one. He wanted to put the quiz show and all the commotion behind him. He told friends that he had made a serious mistake and hoped the hullabaloo would die down. Moe wanted his fans to know him as a good baseball player, not as a freak mental giant.

But the excitement wouldn't go away. Neither the fans nor his teammates would let up. Out on the field, the other players kidded him, shouted questions, or called him "Professor." Moe tried to ignore the questions while he tossed the ball back to the pitchers. He hated the jokes his teammates made while they were warming up. He cared about his batting average, not about being the star of a quiz show.

By 1939, Moe was into his sixteenth year in the majors, having outlasted a lot of other players who started with him. During all those years, there was one person who still refused to come and see him play ball: his father Bernard. Even as an adult, Moe still wanted his father to come to a game, sit in the stands, and watch him catch. But Bernard meant what he had said years earlier. He had not changed his mind. Whenever Moe talked about how much Bernard hated baseball, he also told everyone that he admired his father's stubbornness.

Moe knew most of the other players his age were retiring because they were too old to hit, catch, and run, but he was still clinging to the game. He wanted and needed to stay in baseball. It was his whole life. Nineteen thirty-nine would be Moe's last season in the majors. He couldn't hit much. When he did get into a game, everyone made a big deal over it instead of expecting good catching from an experienced major league catcher. Once in a while he was sent out to catch. As his teammates clapped, whistled, and yelled to cheer him on, he would scramble up from the bullpen, turn his cap backwards, and put on his mask, chest protector, and other gear. He tried to make a joke out of it by asking, "Gentlemen, does everyone still get three strikes out there?" But Moe knew he wasn't fooling anyone. He caught only four times that year.

At the end of that hot summer, the fans crowded into Briggs Stadium in Detroit to watch the Red Sox play the Detroit Tigers. As usual, Moe sat in the dugout sweating out each play. In the fourth inning, Ted Williams and Jim Tabor both hit home runs. Then it was Moe's turn up at the plate.

As the ball raced toward him, he leaned into the bat, and swung hard. The ball sailed into the left field stands. It was the sixth home run of his major league career.

Moe's baseball career ended with that home run in Detroit. He finished the 1939 season with nine hits in thirty-three at bats and with a career batting average of .243. He had played in 663 games. That was enough. He knew he couldn't last forever.

Moe's last game was memorable for more than just his sixth career home run. He would always remember his last game for another important reason. It was played the day before World War II began in Europe.

Moe was worried. His foreign newspapers carried stories of the awful events going on around the world. On September 1, 1939, the Germans invaded Poland. Two days later Great Britain declared war on Germany. The Italian dictator, Benito Mussolini, had sent planes to bomb Ethiopia. In the Pacific, the Japanese had already occupied Manchuria and parts of China.

More and more countries fell to Adolf Hitler and the Nazis. The German dictator seemed unstoppable. Denmark fell in hours, Norway in nine weeks. On May 10, 1940, the Nazis swarmed through the Low Countries. The Netherlands were overrun in five days, Belgium in eighteen days. In only a little more than three weeks, the Nazis drove the British armies out of France. German Panzer divisions outflanked France's strongest defensive fortifications, the Maginot Line. On June 22, the Third French Republic surrendered to Hitler.

Most Americans were shocked, stunned, and surprised, but not Moe. He was angry that the United States was still sitting on the sidelines. He told the reporters traveling with his team that he was sitting in the bullpen while Europe was in flames. But nothing could have been further from the truth. Moe was not telling them everything.

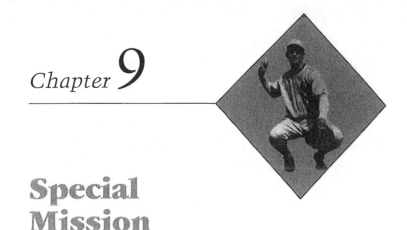

Chapter 9

Special Mission

Moe was furious about what was happening in Germany. The Nazis were building huge bonfires and publicly burning the books they declared unfit to read. These philosophy, history, science, and poetry books were written by some of the world's most brilliant thinkers—all of whom were Jews. This upset Moe because he was a Jew and a scholar who loved learning from books.

When he was asked to give a speech at a book fair, Moe decided to tell people how he felt about the Nazis and their book burning. On October 24, 1940 at the Boston Herald Book Fair, he told the packed audience "...that great ideas would triumph over force. That book burners could not destroy the great thinking found in books." But Moe felt his warnings about

Hitler weren't being taken seriously. Too many people still didn't care. Besides, no one wanted to listen to the bad news.

Moe couldn't wait to get to the Red Sox training camp in Florida, even though he was going to coach in the bullpen, not play. When he finally arrived in Sarasota with the team, everyone was worried about the threat of war. The players were edgy about going into the army, navy, marines, or air corps. Many of the rookies talked about enlisting in the service if the war should come. Moe couldn't shake off his own sense of doom. He had a feeling that something terrible was going to happen and that there was nothing he could do to make it right.

Yet, in the middle of all the awful things that were happening, something good came out of the blue.

That May, the editor of the *Atlantic Monthly* magazine asked Moe to write an article about what it takes to be a good pitcher and a good catcher. Moe was flattered and pleased. This was his chance to tell the world about the game he loved, and about how he felt about being a catcher. Instead of playing ball, now he could write about it. Moe described how he used his big hands, his strong arms, his split second timing, and most of all his brains to make the plays. He wrote about baseball as both an insider playing on the field and as an outsider watching the action from the press box or the stands. That September, the *Atlantic Monthly* printed his article called "Pitchers and Catchers." It would become recognized as one of the best articles ever written about baseball.

At the start of the '42 season, Moe had to do something he never thought he could do. Every major league player had to face it sooner or later. He was thirty-nine years old and he could no longer make the plays. It was time to hang up his uniform and leave the game he loved forever.

Months earlier, in the fall of 1941, Moe put out the word that he wanted a government job. He was still coaching at the spring training camp in Sarasota when a letter arrived from Washington, from the Office of Coordinator of Inter-American Affairs and signed by Nelson A. Rockefeller. Rockefeller asked him to become a goodwill ambassador to Latin America.

It was no secret that the United States and its neighbors south of the border were not getting along. The Nazis were sending stories filled with lies about the United States to radio stations and newspapers in Latin America, which were reporting the stories as news. These stories made the United States look bad and many South Americans who believed the false stories were siding with Germany.

Anxious government officials knew they had to protect the United States from the Nazis. They worried that hostile Nazi sympathizers close to the southern border could sneak across to the United States and make trouble. They worried, too, that American servicemen stationed in Latin America could become targets for sniper fire or bomb attacks.

Rockefeller believed Moe could make friends for the United States and could show that his country wanted to be on good terms with its neighbors. Baseball was a popular sport in Latin America. Moe was a famous major league player who got along easily with people. Rockefeller was sure Moe was a natural choice for this assignment.

Attorney Moe joined the staff of Nelson A. Rockefeller, the Coordinator of Inter-American Affairs. *(Photo courtesy of AP/Wide World Photos.)*

Moe asked for his release from the Red Sox and on January 15, 1942, he announced he was leaving baseball forever. On that same day his father, who had been in poor health, died of cancer. Bernard had never watched a single one of Moe's 633 major league games. Moe would mourn his father by wearing a black tie for the rest of his life.

Moe told newspaper reporters that he was going to Latin America on a special assignment to help the U.S. troops stationed there. News headlines announced, "Berg Leaves Sox to Take Good-Will Ambassador Job." The world believed that Moe was going to South America to talk about baseball and to bring softballs, fishing tackle, records, and books to the men stationed at the U.S. military bases.

But that story was his cover. He had secret orders from Nelson Rockefeller to collect information about the people running Latin American governments, information that could help Washington make friends with them. As he traveled, he was to send back reports about who was friendly to the United States and who was friendly to Germany and Japan.

Moe planned to travel for six months by plane, by jeep, and even on foot through Argentina, Bolivia, Brazil, Colombia, Costa Rica, Cuba, Chile, Ecuador, El Salvador, Guatemala, Haiti, Honduras, Mexico, Nicaragua, Panama, Paraguay, Peru, the Dominican Republic, Uruguay, and Venezuela. It wasn't going to be easy though. People in many of these countries distrusted outsiders, especially North Americans. They believed the lies of the spies, agents, and sympathizers from Germany, Italy, and Japan who were trying to make the United States look bad.

It was all the more dangerous for Moe because weeks earlier, on December 7, 1941, the world war had been brought to American shores. Japanese aircraft bombed Pearl Harbor, the American naval base in Hawaii. Many ships were severely damaged, and some—like the U.S.S. Arizona—were destroyed, with a terrible loss of life.

Along with the rest of his countrymen, Moe was shocked and angry when he heard the news. About the same time, a letter arrived from Washington with his special passport. His trip to Central and South America had become more important than ever. While he waited to start the trip, Moe had an idea that

77

might help stop the war with the Japanese. He would speak to the Japanese in their language and try to convince them to stop fighting. He would ask them to go against the wishes of their government, their warlords, even their emperor.

By the end of February the Office of Strategic Services, the OSS, arranged for him to speak to the Japanese over short-wave radio. On February 24, 1942, Moe went to a Washington radio studio which had a powerful short-wave radio signal that reached halfway around the world to Japan. The broadcast had been arranged by General "Wild Bill" Donovan, head of the Office of Strategic Services. In their language, Moe began to plead with the Japanese people, hoping they could hear him and find it in their hearts to listen to him, and then to act.

I speak to you as a friend of the Japanese people...as one who has studied the origins of your language, your history, your civilization, your progress, your culture and I have found much to admire...We assumed you were civilized even in battle—we thought we saw that when we taught you our national game and watched you play it. We thought that you played and would fight according to rules.

But you have outraged us and every other nation in the world with the exception of two that are tainted with blood, Germany and Italy. They welcome you as friends.

...Believe me when I tell you that you cannot win this war. I am speaking to you as a friend of the Japanese people and tell you to take the reins now. Your warlords are not telling the truth.

The people of the United States and the people of Japan can be friends as they were in the past.

It's up to you.

Moe knew his talk wouldn't stop the killing or the war, but he had to try. The next day his phone rang. The call was from President Franklin Delano Roosevelt in the White House. Speaking for all the American people, President Roosevelt thanked Moe for trying. For Moe, the phone call from the White House was better than hitting a home run in a world series.

Finally, on August 22, 1942, Moe flew to Panama to begin his tour. After he arrived in Latin America, Moe was on his own. He would size up gossip and rumors planted by the Germans, Italians, and Japanese. Then he would decide what could be done to make friends. Rockefeller let Moe make up his mind where to go and what to do. No one knew where Moe would turn up next.

Wherever he traveled, and whichever military bases he visited, Moe usually followed the same schedule. When he arrived, there were invitations waiting, and Moe would decide which ones he wanted to accept. At dinners or parties, beautiful women waited for him to sit or dance with them. Statesmen, generals, and politicians took him aside to talk about their country, the United States, and the war.

Moe spoke Spanish easily and was always full of smiles and charm, as only he could be—when he wanted to be. He told funny jokes, had lots of baseball stories, knew the best wines and the best restaurants. Moe was finding bits and pieces of information everywhere—from diplomats, land owners, reporters, officials, politicians, military men, even their wives and girlfriends. Unsuspected because of his easy-going ways, Moe was searching out the dangers to the United States and writing long, careful reports to Rockefeller marked "SECRET AND CONFIDENTIAL." If Moe was edgy or tired, he never let on. He seemed to soak up energy from doing whatever he was doing because he loved his work.

In Brazil, Moe learned the Portuguese language, and met Brazilian government officials and newspaper reporters. Brazil was important because the United States operated a base in northeast Brazil for U.S. bombers. The American planes would take off from there, heading over the Atlantic Ocean to fight in the African campaigns. Moe was to find out how well-protected the base was from Nazi sympathizers. He also needed to know how the American soldiers stationed there were getting along with the townsfolk. If the soldiers were happy and if the natives liked Americans, then the U.S. bombers and American lives were safe.

While Moe worked hard to make friends, he also worked to improve the life of the American servicemen who found their days long, dull, and boring. He asked Rockefeller to supply movies, baseballs, softballs, volleyballs, basketballs, radios, deep sea fishing tackle, boxing equipment, and libraries for the servicemen to use whenever they had time off. Sometimes he found equipment and materials in local shops and open-air markets, and sometimes he sent for supplies from the States.

Moe wanted Latin Americans to become true friends of the United States instead of suspicious neighbors. The best way to teach democracy, he believed, was through the schools and the universities. Moe wanted to use education to make a change for the better, just as his parents and family used education to improve their lives. He insisted that the United States offer to teach democracy in Latin American classrooms. Moe also suggested that the United States soldiers learn about the history and geography of the countries they were stationed in, and learn to understand the customs and laws of the local people. Language classes, he said, should be held for the officers and enlisted men so they could talk to the natives.

After six months, satisfied that his assignment in Latin America was over, Moe packed his bags, paid his last hotel bill, made a few phone calls, and boarded a plane for home.

The crew closed the door and the plane taxied to the end of the runway. There was a deepening roar from the engines as the plane moved faster and faster, a silhouette in the gathering gloom. Then its nose pointed to the United States, drifting upward, still climbing. Moe leaned back and relaxed, preparing for the questions waiting for him about the dangers in Latin America and what the Axis was doing.

There was a note waiting for him at his Washington hotel from Nelson Rockefeller.

...I want to take this opportunity to tell you how much I appreciate all you've done for this office and for the government. Your work in assisting the army to orient more effectively their units in South America to the various local problems has contributed greatly to inter-American programs.

Only someone with your experience and knowledge of international, as well as human, problems could have handled this situation with such tact and effectiveness.

Congratulations and very best wishes.

Sincerely,
Nelson

Chapter 10

The Spy Game

Although Moe didn't realize it, the flight back to North America was the first leg of a journey that was to take him through World War II.

When he got back to Washington it was early February 1943. Moe wasn't sure what he would do next. He told his influential friends that he was available to go to work right away. Moe closed out his mission to the Southern Hemisphere with a sixty-page, single-spaced report that took him until the end of the month to finish.

Thorough down to the last detail, Moe told Nelson Rockefeller the inside story of what was going on in Central and South America. He reported which officials were friendly to the Allies and what governments were sympathetic to the Axis. He explained how the United States should go about making friends.

After finishing his report, Moe received a telephone call from a lawyer who had once worked with him at Satterlee and Canfield and also knew him from Princeton. He asked Moe to join an important new top-secret government team. It was with a group called the Office of Strategic Services. His friend told him no one was to know anything about the call.

The man responsible for the offer was General William "Wild Bill" Donovan. In 1939, President Roosevelt, convinced the United States needed its own spy network to protect itself from its enemies, ordered Donovan to set up a spy organization for the United States.

The president understood that, in 1939, the United States was the only major world power without its own peacetime secret agents. "Wild Bill" Donovan's job was to organize the first peacetime civilian under-cover spy organization in the history of the United States. This was the Office of Strategic Services, which everyone would later call the OSS.

Moe learned that Donovan had worked fast. Across the Atlantic, all of Europe was in danger of being con-quered by the dictators. Donovan had to quickly build a spy network that could stand up to Hitler's skillful, expert, well-trained, and experienced secret agents. Yet all he had in the beginning were new, inexperienced, unpracticed, and raw recruits. Donovan had created his team of spies from men and women who were pro-fessors, gangsters, sports stars, lawyers, housewives, actors, soldiers, and more. Although they came from different backgrounds, they understood Donovan ex-pected them all to be closemouthed and clever.

Moe was a natural for the OSS. His years as a baseball player had given him a powerful body with strong arms, plenty of endurance, and lots of energy. The many languages he had studied for the love of it were now important to him as a spy. He could speak Hebrew, Japanese, Greek, French, Yiddish, Spanish, Portuguese and German. His ear could pick up the slightest change of accent. When he spoke a foreign language, he sounded as if he had lived in that country all his life.

From the days when he took pictures of foreign installations without being noticed or caught, Moe knew how to make himself fade into the background. Wearing ordinary clothes, he could blend into a crowd. His travels all over the world had taught him how to get around in a strange place. He could arrive anywhere in Europe, Japan, or South America and find his destination without asking directions or calling attention to himself.

But there was one more piece of Moe's life that made him especially useful as an undercover agent. Moe was a loner. He didn't have a wife and he wasn't permanently involved with a girlfriend. There was no one with whom he stayed in close touch. He had always lived alone, traveled alone, and best of all, enjoyed being alone.

For all these reasons, Donovan had decided he wanted Moe in the OSS. To him, Moe was the perfect spy. As for Moe, although he loved being a famous baseball star and reading stories about himself in the newspapers, this time he couldn't tell the reporters or anyone else what he was about to do.

Soon Moe discovered that training for the OSS was just as tough as getting into condition for the majors. In early August, after signing a contract, he and the other recruits spent weeks in a secret OSS boot camp hidden in Maryland. Throughout the training, Moe made himself keep up with the youngest OSS recruits.

He learned how to use pistols and rifles, break open safes, and blow up bridges. Moe learned to fight hand to hand like a commando. He practiced jumping from a plane, then landing, rolling, releasing his chute harness, and sprinting for cover. He studied the quickest way to surprise the enemy and to kill without making a sound.

When the course was finished, Moe took a vow to be loyal to the United States and pledged never to tell about the OSS. Then he signed for his revolver and received his capsules of potassium cyanide, a poison that kills instantly when swallowed, so that he could commit suicide if he were captured. Agents were expected to kill themselves to avoid being tortured into giving up important secrets to the enemy. Moe was ready for action.

But first he faced an important decision. Should he become part of the military or remain a civilian? Many other OSS agents were joining the army and becoming commissioned officers. Moe could also have a high rank as an army officer if he wanted one.

On future spy missions, his life could depend on the choice he needed to make now. If he were captured behind enemy lines while wearing civilian clothes, he would be considered a spy and couldn't be protected by the international rules for taking soldiers as prisoners. If he were not shot immediately, he would probably need to swallow the cyanide pills to avoid torture. Even so, the choice was easy for Moe. He decided to remain a civilian. He didn't want to take orders from anyone if he didn't have to.

Years later Moe would tell how the orders for his first undercover assignment came quickly. Donovan personally picked Moe to get into the heart of Yugoslavia, find out what was going on there, and send the information back to the United States. Moe packed his equipment and quietly slipped out of Washington to an airport and boarded an army transport.

Yugoslavia had been filled with Nazis since being captured by the German armies on April 6, 1941. On that day Nazi soldiers, tanks, and planes tore through the paralyzed country from all directions—from Germany, Hungary, Romania, and Bulgaria. As the country was overrun, Yugoslavia's King Peter, a teenager, hastily escaped to England for safety.

From the day their country fell, Yugoslavian patriots had held out against the Nazis in their own guerrilla war. They blew up railroad tracks, destroyed telephone lines, killed soldiers, and did whatever they could to slow down the German war machine. But even while they were fighting the hated Nazis, two groups of Yugoslavian resistance fighters were battling each other. One group, still loyal to the king, were the Cherniks headed by General Draza Mihailovic, a Serbian. The other group, wanting the power passed to the people, were the partisans headed by a Croatian named Josip Broz, who was also known as "Tito."

Even though both groups were fighting the same enemies, the Germans and Italians, they were also killing each other. The battles between the resistance fighters were just as fierce and bloody as those they fought against the Germans and Italians. Both factions, Moe knew, were begging the United States for money, guns, and supplies. Before the United States would send money it had to decide which partisan group would be victorious. It wanted to back the winner and it was Moe's job to figure out what was going on.

There wasn't anyone to help Moe and there wasn't much information to go on. Only a few U.S. secret agents had ever managed to get inside Yugoslavia.

Slipping behind German lines, Moe arrived in Yugoslavia in the blazing heat of August 1943. As he traveled the tangled network of mountain ranges and valleys, he knew hidden resistance fighters watched his every move. Wherever he went, Moe came face to face with a country destroyed by fighting. Whole villages had disappeared, the people machine-gunned down or burned out.

Moe was used to fierce competition. He had seen it on the baseball diamond, even in business, but it was nothing like the competition and the hatred he discovered between the two groups of Yugoslav resistance fighters. Even while they were being terrorized by the Nazis they both hated, the two groups of Yugoslav resistance fighters were tearing each other apart.

That summer Moe climbed his way up the mountains to the headquarters of each resistance group's hideout. He went first to General Mihailovic's camp hidden high in the steep hills. The pair talked and while they did, Moe looked around the camp and took in everything. Leaving Mihailovic, he inched his way over steep cliffs across the mountains, on the back roads and hidden paths to the other camp, where he talked to Tito's aides.

Moe had to choose one side over the other. In baseball, his job had once been to pick the best rookies and to scout the strongest players. Once again he had to pick out the future winners. Moe calmly considered the two resistance forces who were furiously fighting each other. As usual he thought about everything very carefully. Finally Moe made up his mind, choosing Tito's men because he believed they were better fighters and had the support of more Yugoslavians.

In his usual, careful way Moe wrote a report, which was smuggled out to Donovan in Washington. He told how Yugoslavia was tearing itself apart and how the two groups of resistance fighters were destroying each other. He knew the reports were being read by people 3,000 miles away, across the Atlantic Ocean. But Moe knew that the American readers could not imagine the horror unless they saw it for themselves.

Most of that summer, Moe wrote more reports to Washington from Yugoslavia. He had to wait on the sidelines while the United States government made up its mind. By the time the government decided to be friends to both groups, Tito was already receiving support from the Communists and the Soviet Union. It hadn't turned out the way he wanted, but Moe was not discouraged. He waited for his next assignment.

At the end of the summer, Moe's new orders arrived from Washington. He was to return through German lines to OSS headquarters in London. When he left Yugoslavia, the Soviet armies were already marching into the country to fight the Nazis. From London he flew to Washington to report to General Donovan.

Wartime Washington was filled with men and women in uniforms from all over the world. As a civilian he stood out in the crowds moving through the city. The hotels were overcrowded. Many travelers slept sitting up in hotel lobby chairs. Moe returned to the Mayflower Hotel where he usually lived. The desk clerk quickly gave him keys to one of the better rooms, while other travelers patiently waited in line for just a cot. Moe unpacked his bag, made a few phone calls, then sat back to wait for what was going to happen next.

Near the end of that year, Moe received the call he'd been hoping for. The OSS wanted him in on a new top-secret plan. It didn't have anything to do with guns, or tanks, or anything else men had ever used to kill each other. This new weapon was coming from the world of science. Moe didn't know much about science. He had tried to stay away from science in high school and in college. He was much better at languages and baseball. But this new idea was coming from physicists who wanted to build a weapon that sounded as if it came out of science fiction.

At first Moe was puzzled. He was a baseball player. He knew lots of languages, loved going to parties, liked to tell good stories. He'd been a radio star and a lawyer, but he certainly was not a scientist or a mathematician. What good could he do? Why did a team of government physicists want him?

What was going to happen next would turn out to be the surprise play of the war.

And of Moe's life.

Chapter 11

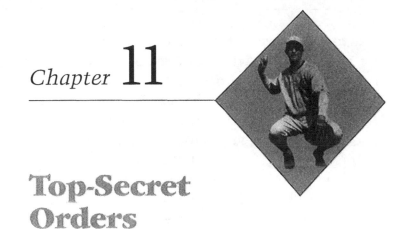

Top-Secret Orders

Late in 1943, Moe joined a brand new project that hardly a dozen people in all the United States knew about in full detail. It was hidden from civilians at home, from the military, even from Harry Truman, vice president of the United States.

At top-secret meetings in Washington, Moe listened as scientists and military experts talked about the development of a new weapon that would help the Allies win the war. At the same time, the Nazis were publishing news stories about their own new, secret weapon, which, they boasted, could blow up an entire city. Scientists and refugees who escaped from Europe brought their own stories about this frightening instrument of war. There were even rumors that the Nazis planned to use South America, dangerously close to the United States, as a base for this new monster weapon. The German news stories were filled with just enough scientific facts to suggest that the Nazi secret weapon could be real. But no one in the United States knew for certain whether the stories were true or were made up to frighten the Allies.

Moe set out to learn what he could about the American and Nazi secret weapons. Once again, he became a student as he hunted down the information. He learned that while he had been busy playing baseball, the world of science had gone though a major change in its thinking. In 1933, while Moe had been caught up in the very first major league All-Star Game, a revolution in physics had begun in a laboratory in Italy, where Dr. Enrico Fermi, the Italian physicist, was studying the basic structure of atoms.

A team of German scientists at Berlin's Kaiser Wilhelm Institute eagerly read Fermi's research report in 1934. Otto Hahn, the laboratory director and his two assistants, Lise Meitner and Fritz Strassmann, were also studying the basic structure of atoms, including how to bombard them with neutrons. The German team wanted to create a chain reaction. In their experiments, they planned to use the energy liberated by one "smashed" atom as a "match" to "ignite" the next atom.

But the Berlin scientific team found itself caught up in world events on the brink of World War II. Suddenly, Lise Meitner became "undesirable" by Nazi racial standards because she came from a Jewish family. Fearing she would be arrested if she did not leave Germany, Lise Meitner escaped from Berlin and headed for Stockholm, Sweden. It was a neutral country where she hoped she could live without fear.

Soon after she arrived in Stockholm, Dr. Meitner changed her thinking about her research results in Berlin. She realized that the Berlin team had discovered a way to change matter into energy. Lise Meitner was the very first to understand what her partners in Germany and all the other physicists did not grasp—the inside of the atom, the nucleus itself, could be torn apart.

Lise Meitner sent her report to the British scientific magazine, *Nature.* Her article, entitled "Disintegration of Uranium by Neutrons: A New Type of Nuclear Reaction" appeared on February 11, 1939. Her ideas would transform the history of the world forever. Scientists all over the world immediately understood that Lise Meitner's discovery made it possible to develop a bomb more deadly than any weapon ever known.

At the same time, war was on everyone's mind. The Nazis were pushing their anti-Jewish program and had marched into Poland. Italy had invaded Albania, Russia had taken over Finland, and Japan was waging an undeclared war in China. After he read Dr. Meitner's article, Niels Bohr, head of the Technical Institute in Copenhagen, Denmark, rushed to the United States to visit Professor Enrico Fermi. The Italian researcher had escaped from Italy and was now a professor at Columbia University in New York City. Bohr and Fermi traveled to Princeton University to talk over Lise Meitner's idea with Professor Albert Einstein, also a refugee.

The three scientists agreed that the enormous energy Lise Meitner wrote about made an atomic weapon clearly possible. They insisted on a special, private meeting with President Roosevelt. In it they carefully explained to the president how and why it was possible to develop an atomic weapon. They warned the president that Hitler's Germany was already developing this deadly weapon and that Europe's only uranium supplies, used for the bomb's fuel, were in mines controlled by Germany. Even worse, by late 1939, there was a race between German, Italian, and English scientists to see who could build the first atomic weapon.

President Roosevelt listened closely. Then he acted quickly and quietly. Early in 1940 a top-secret atomic program was started in the United States. At the same time the few American scientists and spies already in on the secret desperately tried to find out if the enemy really knew how to build an atomic weapon and if so, how far ahead of the United States they really were.

While Moe had been on other spy missions, the army, navy, marines and air corps had sent their secret agents to Europe and to Japan to search for evidence of the enemy's hidden atomic research. But the bits and pieces of undercover information the Americans found didn't make much sense. Too many different spies were reporting to too many different bosses.

Finally, in the fall of 1943, the American services organized one secret spy team for the United States, carefully picking the best people from the armed forces and from Donovan's OSS team. These Americans would have to sneak into Europe, search for enemy scientists and their laboratories, and follow the trail of the Axis atomic weapon program. Then it was up to General Donovan to pick his best agent from that group to move ahead of the others into enemy territory. General Donovan knew the perfect under-cover man for this dangerous job: Moe Berg.

What made Moe so special to Donovan? The General knew Moe was bright and questioned every-thing. Moe was a fast learner. What Moe didn't know, he would find someone to teach him, or teach him-self. And most important to Donovan, Moe could be counted on to keep his mouth shut, figure a way out of tight spots, and get the job done.

When Moe got news of his important, mysterious assignment, he realized he had to learn physics, math-ematics, and chemistry, fast. He had to learn about this mysterious science full of strange new atomic ideas. He would have to think like the enemy scien-tists who were feverishly working on the enemy's dreaded atomic weapon.

Over the years, when his old buddies and friends asked, "What are you doing these days?" Moe would put his finger to this lips and say, "S-h-h-h." It was as if it were a game, a dark secret. Moe never, ever gave anyone a straight answer. Or if he did, it amounted to no answer at all.

Now, with Donovan's orders, he couldn't let out-siders suspect what his hidden life was all about. Every day Moe put on his dark business suit, black tie, white drip-dry shirt, read his newspapers, and took notes. No one would have guessed that he was on the way to some important, secret meeting or that he now had a new code name, "the Black-Haired Boy."

Chapter 12

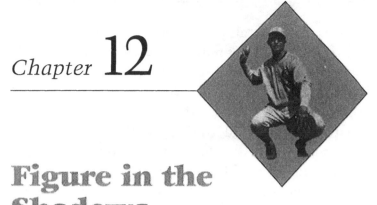

Figure in the Shadows

Moe's life changed. He began to learn names like Einstein and Fermi. His new acquaintances were no longer athletes, Hollywood movie stars, or language professors, but the world's best researchers, engineers, science professors, and military experts. He started to learn mathematics, chemistry, and physics.

Surprisingly, science came easily to him. When he was growing up, his parents told him that his older brother Sam was the scientific brain in the family. Moe was always the ballplayer who was good in languages. It amazed him that he was catching on so fast and with so little trouble.

As the war went on, every newspaper and radio in Europe continued to spread the story of Germany's new atomic wonder weapon. These enemy stories were propaganda, clearly meant to frighten the Allies. Moe understood that many Americans feared that the Nazi boasts and bragging were true.

Before long, Moe and the Washington military realized what American scientists already knew—that the mastermind behind the dreaded German atomic weapon was Werner Heisenberg, a genius who was considered the world's greatest applied physicist. Officially, he was a professor at the University of Leipzig. But American scientists and Allied secret agents knew Heisenberg was the key to the German atomic secrets and was directing the Nazi atomic bomb program.

Moe and the OSS learned from resistance fighters that Werner Heisenberg was working in a small, quiet town somewhere in southern Germany. Allied air raids on German cities had forced him to move his atomic research laboratories into the countryside. While Moe waited to begin his work in Europe, he was assigned a new partner and given a new coded spy name.

While General Donovan and the OSS worked with Moe, General Leslie R. Groves put together yet another team of American secret agents to search for enemy scientists and German atomic weapons. This other team was called the Alsos Mission. As he set up the Alsos Mission, General Groves talked over his idea with General Donovan. The generals believed that by sending out two spy teams to find the same information they might learn twice as much. And just as important, if one group was captured by the enemy, they had another team to find out what the Allies needed to know.

Moe and his partner got their orders from Donovan. They were going to sneak into Italy as soon as it was captured by the Americans, find important Italian rocket scientists, kidnap them, and bring them to the United States by submarine. Donovan's plan, called Project Larson, was to use captured Italian scientists to lead U.S. agents to German atomic scientists still working in hidden laboratories.

Moe's part in Project Larson had a new secret code name, AZUSA, which stood for "A to Z, United States of America." The people in charge of these top-secret spy missions didn't tell Alsos about Moe and AZUSA, or tell Moe about Alsos. They believed the fewer people who knew the plans, the better.

While waiting for his orders to leave for Europe, Moe learned about the parts of the atom and the theories about the process of splitting the atom, called fission. He gathered information from reading textbooks and from talking to experimenters, engineers, college professors, and refugee scientists from European universities and technical schools. He visited laboratories where experiments were being done that might help him understand atomic physics.

Still, Moe had too much time on his hands. He bounced around for most of that winter—traveling to New York to see friends, dating, going to meetings, visiting with his family, reading his reports and journals, and waiting.

He made more lists of the scientists he was to hunt down. He learned about the elements uranium and thorium. He wanted to be ready to search out the supplies of these rare metals hidden in Europe. He dutifully practiced making clear diagrams of enemy anti-aircraft defenses, of buildings, even making his own blueprints of the Nazis' suspected new headquarters and laboratories.

Moe made some new friends in Washington, but he never got too close to any of them. As usual, he liked to do his own thing, alone. Still, there wasn't much Moe could do but wait for his orders from General Donovan.

Moe was invited to attend more top-secret briefings. At these meetings with scientists and military officers he always took long, detailed, careful notes. Moe had learned there were three important parts to building an atomic bomb—the right scientists, the right fuel (uranium or thorium), and the right laboratory.

By December 1943, Moe was aching for action. In early December, the State Department got permission for him to travel to Britain, Cairo, and Algiers. One day slid to another, but Moe still sat in Washington, waiting for final orders. The OSS had a slogan for it: "Here today. Here tomorrow." And yet waiting around wasn't new to Moe. He'd sat on the bench in major league games in just the same way.

Over the winter Moe continued to carefully collect bits of news and information on the German and Italian atomic scientists he planned to hunt down in Europe. He found out about their families and their children. He learned who their friends were and what their hobbies were. Most of all, he found out if they had faith in Hitler's plan to conquer Europe, or if they were friendly to the Allies. He was putting together the kind of file most spies made before going out on a mission. Moe planned to use this information about the lives of enemy scientists to track them down and quickly become their friends.

By the end of January, Moe's partner was transferred. This was better for Moe, who always liked to work alone. The winter snows slowly began to melt. The buds on the cherry trees announced it was spring.

Almost everyone around Moe was overworked, rushing around, about to leave Washington, or just returning, while Moe still waited for orders. In his usual slouch hat, trench coat, dark business suit, and black tie, Moe went to more scientific meetings and OSS briefings. He always carried his small black notebook and took careful notes, just as if he was a student in a classroom. This was a habit by now. He listened carefully as they told him what he should look for, find out, and send back.

One day, Major Robert Furman from the Army Corps of Engineers called Moe into his office. Furman, General Groves' right-hand man repeated that General Groves wanted Moe to find Italian scientists and let them lead him to Heisenberg and to the secret German atomic bomb laboratories. The Allies had to know whether the Germans were lying about their atomic weapon or whether the Germans were really building one. But even though Furman and Groves desperately wanted him to leave, they couldn't send Moe to Europe until the American Fifth Army, commanded by General Mark Clark, was in control of the Italian front. The OSS needed permission from General Clark's office to send Moe to Italy. But permission was slow in coming because the Americans had not yet reclaimed Rome.

It was almost May when Major Furman wanted to see Moe again. Moe opened his black notebook and carefully took notes as Furman gave him his assignment. Moe was to find out how strong the German atomic weapon project was, and how much damage the Allied bombs had done to Werner Heisenberg's laboratory in Berlin-Dahliem. Furman handed Moe a list of enemy scientists with a number next to each name. The number told Moe how important each man was for him to investigate. And last, Furman wanted Moe to report on any hidden supplies of rare metals the enemy might have for their atomic bomb research.

Furman repeated that the mission was top-secret, and Moe assured the major that he understood. Finally, Furman gave Moe his travel orders. He was to leave in early May, and go first to London, then Portugal, Algiers, and finally Italy. Furman saw to it that Moe had a lot of U.S. money to take with him—about two thousand dollars. In Europe, American money was as good as gold. It would let Moe buy favors, live well, and bribe his way across the continent.

On May 4, Moe went to a military airplane hangar near Washington, D.C. As he boarded the four-engine plane, he carried his expense money, a .45 pistol and his secret cyanide pills. Most of his fellow passengers for that long flight were wearing uniforms. In his civilian suit, Moe looked like a war correspondent—at least that's what he wanted people to think, but his orders were signed by General Donovan himself. The General didn't usually sign travel orders; most of the time someone on his staff took care of the routine paper work. But this was a very important and extraordinary mission.

The plane took off, circled the field, and began the long climb up. Moe settled back for the overseas flight to London. A lot of people had worked long and hard to get him started. Now it was going to be up to him.

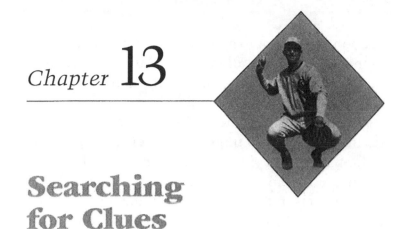

Chapter 13

Searching for Clues

London had changed dramatically since Moe's last visit; marks of German bombing were everywhere. People lived in dread of the next German bomb attack. Yet the nightly air raids had become part of London life, like the community sing-alongs every night in the air-raid shelters. Sandbags were piled high outside all the important public buildings, including Parliament and the Waterloo train station. People casually carried their gas masks slung over one shoulder as if they were book bags.

The OSS office was in the heart of London. Moe reported to Donovan at the OSS, his paycheck came from the OSS, and he used secret OSS couriers to send his reports to Washington, but he was really working for both Donovan and Groves. Moe used his OSS con-

nection as a screen to hide his more important assignment: to find out all he could about Germany's
atomic bomb program and then report directly to
General Groves.

Moe hung around the OSS office for a few weeks,
taking notes at meetings about secret weapons and
talking to people. If he thought they could help him,
he invited them to lunch or dinner. Everything in
London was rationed, but Moe managed to find
restaurants still serving portions of good food. A filling meal, accompanied by his stories about baseball,
Hollywood stars, and the president of the United
States, usually changed strangers into friends.

Bit by bit Moe put together a picture about the new
atomic bomb. He met with Dr. H. P. Robertson, an
American, who had been a mathematics professor at
Princeton University and now worked for the Office
of Scientific Research and Development. What Moe
hadn't already learned from the other physicists back
in the States, he learned from Robertson in London.

He also met Colonel H. K. Calvert, the man picked
by General Groves to serve as his special European
representative. Calvert's job was to read the secret
reports from spies all over the world that arrived in
London every day. He sorted through information
from refugees, captured enemy scientists, escaped
prisoners of war, and anyone else who knew anything
about the Nazis and their atomic bomb, searching for
clues about the secret weapons program.

Soon Moe was working alongside Calvert, plowing
through the bulky stacks of reports to confirm which
top German atomic scientists might know the location of Germany's hidden laboratories. Professor

Werner Heisenberg, the Nobel Prize winner, was always at the top of his list. Heisenberg's name was closely followed by others, including Professor Max von Laue, also a Nobel Prize winner; Professor Walter Gerlach; Dr. Kurt Diebner, who was in charge of building Germany's uranium reactor; Professor Paul Hartec and Dr. Erich Bagge, who were doing research on uranium isotopes; and Dr. Otto Hahn, who had been Lise Meitner's boss.

Whenever he took time off from his search, Moe walked through London. He loved the city's museums and libraries, and he poked around its bookshops filled with old, rare books about languages. On Sundays Moe walked fifteen to twenty miles, crossing from one section of London to another. As he made his way through the city he saw holes, craters, and piles of bricks that once were homes and buildings.

In spite of the brutal bombings, Moe found crowds of children playing in the streets and parks. Many London families had sent their sons and daughters away from London to escape the German bombs. These children went to the country or even as far away as America to live with other families until the war was over. Still, there were many children who spent their nights sleeping in air-raid shelters and then emerged at daylight to continue life as usual.

While Moe was in London, the huge Allied armada crossed the English Channel to France and hit the German-held beaches. The Normandy invasion in June 1944 was the bloody beginning of Hitler's end. While Allied troops fought their way from the beaches of Normandy through France, other Allied troops inched their way along the southern coast of the Mediterranean. Using Sicily as a steppingstone to Italy, the Allies forced the Italians to surrender. That June, General Mark Clark's weary army struggled into Rome.

United States secret agents were waiting impatiently for the capture of Rome. As soon as the Allies entered the city, Moe left England to follow Clark's advancing army into Italy.

Moe knew that General Groves wanted certain Italian scientists rushed back to the United States as soon as possible. But he wasn't aware that the secret Alsos team of undercover agents was also racing to contact the same enemy scientists. Their job, like Moe's, was to capture Italian scientists and their secret papers and to find Germany's atomic research laboratories.

As Moe and other OSS agents rushed into Italy, the Alsos team, headed by Colonel Boris Pash, was also moving quickly into Rome, where Italy's best scientists had been living and working with the Nazis. Despite the fierce fighting around Rome, the Germans had not bombed or torched the city because they considered it a place of culture.

In Rome, Moe found a jumble of screaming crowds, thundering tanks, and American infantry. German sharpshooters and snipers were still firing as they ran away from the advancing American army. Many Italians welcomed the Allies, even though Italy had been Germany's ally. Moe went to one of Rome's best hotels, and, although it was filled, he managed to get a room. He then began his search for Edoardo Amaldi, Italy's top researcher experimenting with fission.

Dr. Amaldi lived with his wife, Ginestra, and their children, on the Via Parioli near the University of

Rome, where he taught at the Physics Institute. Moe knew he had to reach Amaldi quickly, before anyone else found him or tried to question him.

In army intelligence it was often said, "You don't know what you don't know." Perhaps Amaldi would give him fresh information. Still, Moe couldn't be sure if Amaldi would speak openly with him. If Amaldi did talk, could Moe trust him? Would he lie or mislead Moe with false information? Moe believed the researcher was friendly to the Allies, even though he had remained in Rome during the war.

It was no secret that everyone in Rome was hungry, thanks to the war. Moe loaded up with chocolates and coffee, put on a fresh white nylon shirt and black tie, and told his army driver to take him to the Via Parioli. When Signora Amaldi faced Moe in the door of her house, Moe could see that she was not surprised to find a strange American asking to see her husband. Moe learned for the first time about Boris Pash and the Alsos team and was told that they had already been there.

After bringing greetings from Fermi, Moe listened as Professor Amaldi explained to Moe that he was already under orders from the United States government. Boris Pash had ordered Amaldi to stay in Rome. But Moe's orders were clear; he was to help Dr. Amaldi reach the United States, where General Groves, the OSS, and the American scientists could question him. Amaldi, who was given two different stories and two different orders from two men representing the same government, appeared confused, annoyed, even angry. To make things right, Moe backed off and left. He first had to reassure Professor Amaldi and then get him to talk.

The next day Moe went to Amaldi's house and waited for him to return home for lunch. When the professor arrived, Moe dismissed the idea of Amaldi going to the United States or even to Naples for questioning by the OSS. Moe invited the professor to a dinner of meat and pasta. As they dined, Moe carefully guided the conversation to what he needed to find out. Did Amaldi know where Werner Heisenberg was hiding? How far along were the Germans in building the atomic bomb? Where were their laboratories?

Amaldi's answers were not what Moe had hoped for. The professor hadn't worked on fission research since 1941 because the University of Rome didn't have the necessary equipment. But Amaldi did confirm the names of the two German scientists who were heading the Nazi research—Otto Hahn and Werner Heisenberg.

Moe still wasn't satisfied with the information. He wanted the professor to leave Rome. He continued to visit the professor, bringing more chocolates, candy, coffee, and cigarettes. Finally, Professor Amaldi told Moe he would be willing to go to the United States for a reasonable length of time.

After arranging for Amaldi and his family to leave for the States, Moe decided to contact another Italian scientist, Gian Carlo Wick, who had been Enrico Fermi's assistant. Wick had taken Fermi's place at the University of Rome, after Fermi's escape to the United States.

Moe found the Italian physicist and treated him to a generous dinner. Just as he had done with Amaldi, he gently guided the talk over dinner to the Germans and their atomic bomb project. Dr. Wick hadn't done any

108

atomic research himself, but he had seen Werner Heisenberg. It was Wick's opinion that Werner Heisenberg didn't like what Adolf Hitler was doing. On the other hand Heisenberg appeared to be loyal to Germany.

Wick thought Heisenberg was living and working in southern Germany near a forest, but told Moe he was not sure about the address. Moe suspected Wick knew exactly where Werner Heisenberg was hiding, but wouldn't tell because he was afraid the Allies would hurt Heisenberg. Then Wick added that, every now and then, he received mail from Heisenberg. In fact, he brought with him a postcard from Heisenberg dated mid-January 1944—six months earlier.

Not wanting to push too hard, Moe listened as Wick tried to show how difficult life was for Heisenberg. His postcard told how his family was barely surviving the Allied bombing. His laboratory, the Leipzig Institute, had been destroyed, but the Berlin Institute was still standing. Moe half listened as he planned what he had to do. When Wick showed Moe the postcard, he noticed the postmark; Heisenberg had mailed it from Heckingen, a village in the Black Forest. Although Heisenberg was still safely behind German lines and out of reach, Moe had to tell General Groves what he had found.

Meanwhile, as Moe was searching for the Italian scientists in and around Rome, the war was furiously going on all around him. German snipers were still shooting from hidden attics. Blasts of Allied machine gun fire were picking off retreating Nazi sharpshooters. Italian guerrilla fighters were tracking down stray German soldiers.

As soon as the Allies liberated an area, Moe went in right behind the troops. He talked to more Italian scientists, engineers, and technicians. He went through their files and studied their maps. He found out about secret weapons and equipment, and advanced Italian research in aeronautics, rockets, and jet engines. He dug out hidden reports on germ warfare, chemical weapons, and poison gas.

Moe reported all that he had seen and heard to Donovan's office. He added enemy blueprints, microfilms and records, and told about the scientific work done by the Italian researchers. Though he couldn't speak Italian fluently, he could read well enough to translate scientific reports and files.

Moe sent secret cables across the Atlantic. He made sure his detailed reports traveled in the best OSS pouches, carried by the most trusted secret OSS couriers. Some of the information Washington already knew, but Moe uncovered many new facts because he alone tracked down the files.

By the time Moe finished his assignment, nothing was left out. General Donovan and General Groves sent word that Moe had provided the most useful information about fission and Italian research that they ever had.

During the summer of 1944, Moe learned more details about the unspeakable Nazi cruelty to the Jews. Stories from the underground told what the Nazis were doing to annihilate the Jews. Many Italian Jews had been hauled off, packed in sealed freight railroad cars, and sent to Nazi work camps or concentration death camps. Moe reported these horror stories to General Donovan and to General Groves along with his other dispatches.

But Moe's orders were to search for the German atomic scientists and to find out how far the Germans had developed their atomic bomb program. It was this information, Moe knew, that would help the Allies crush the German war machine and end the war. Still, Moe made up his own list of the top Nazi party members who were in charge of exterminating the Jews. After questioning scientists, resistance fighters, and the underground, he put together his own private file. After the war, perhaps, he could help bring the Nazi murderers to justice.

After the Americans liberated Rome, Moe and other OSS officers were granted an audience with Pope Pius XII at the Vatican. Moe decided to use the visit to plead for his fellow Jews. During his audience with the pope, Moe appealed to the pontiff in halting Italian. He asked the pope to tell the world the Vatican was against what the Germans were doing to the Jews. The pope listened to Moe, but he did not act.

Moe couldn't know it then, but after the war the men on his list would be brought to trial for their war crimes with General Donovan assisting the prosecution. Moe would be invited to sit in the courtroom in Nuremberg, Germany, and watch as the Nazis were tried, convicted, and sentenced.

Chapter 14

Finding Answers

The rest of the summer Moe stayed near the front, keeping only a half step behind the fighting as the Allies advanced through Italy. The armed forces were moving forward to Florence, a city in central Italy on the Arno River. Although Italy had formally surrendered, many German troops still remained in Italy, determined to kill as many Allied soldiers as they could before they were captured.

While this fierce fighting was going on, the two teams of American agents raced each other in search of Italian scientists. At the same time, German patrols were hunting down the same scientists. The researchers were hard to find because many of them had disappeared during the war to join the Allied resistance forces or to become guerrilla fighters.

As Moe questioned the captured scientists and went through their files, one name, Antonio Ferri, kept coming up. Ferri was classified simply as an aeronautical engineer. Trusting a hunch, Moe decided to find out more about him.

It turned out Ferri had been experimenting with high-speed flight. One of the world's brightest engineers, he'd been in charge of developing a wind tunnel which simulated speeds of almost twenty-five hundred miles an hour. This new fast speed was called "supersonic flight."

It was clear to Moe that whoever had the fastest plane would rule the skies. And whoever ruled the skies would win the war. He knew Germany and England were already developing supersonic airplanes, but the United States was far behind. If Moe could track down Ferri and persuade him to come to the United States, then America would be able to catch up and perhaps beat the others in the race to build supersonic war planes.

Other undercover agents reported that there was a price on Ferri's head. Moe learned Nazi agents had orders to kidnap him and carry him off to Germany, or to kill him. German patrols were combing the hills and the countryside to find him. The British and Russians were also moving in. Agents from those countries were on their way to convince Ferri to go to England or to Russia. Whoever found Ferri first would have one of the greatest prizes of the war. Time was running out.

Moe joined the hunt. When he finally found the Ferri house, it looked as if it had long been deserted. The family had disappeared. He searched the house for clues and looked at old records. He talked to friends and neighbors and listened carefully and patiently. Finally an off-hand remark led him to Ferri's mother-in-law, Signora Cina Mola, who lived in Rome. It didn't take long for Moe to convince the woman to trust him and tell him what he had come to find out. Signora Mola told him that Ferri had disappeared into the Apennine hills north of Rome to join the resistance fighters. Ferri, his brother, and his father were sharpshooters helping the Allies fight the Germans.

Guided by Italian partisans, Moe trekked deep into the woods and finally found Ferri hidden in the shadows of the forest. Since Ferri was a friend to the Allies, Moe hoped he could count on him. The two men liked each other instantly. Ferri's wife, Renata, and three young children were close by. Moe quickly became a good friend to the Ferri family. While Moe played baseball with the children, Ferri gathered his reports and scientific information. He turned the records of his experiments over to Moe, who sent them on to Washington. The records contained flight test information, blueprints of the wind tunnel where they made the tests, and reports of what Ferri had seen while visiting the German top-secret flight laboratories. Furman shot back a reply from Washington: "Deliver Ferri to the United States as soon as possible."

It took a few weeks for Moe to convince him, but by September, Ferri and his family had left for the United States. With Ferri's help, the United States would be able to build supersonic airplanes.

By mid-August, the Allied infantry had pushed back the Germans and freed Florence. Moe was right behind the advancing American army, who were right on the heels of the retreating Germans. As his jeep bumped along the American lines, Moe could hear the rifles and machine guns of partisan sharpshooters picking off the lingering German snipers.

He crossed the Ponte Vecchio, the famous bridge, into the heart of Florence, a city of artistic masterpieces and beautiful architecture. As usual, he went directly to the city's best hotel, the Excelsior, and managed to get a room. Inside the hotel's crystal and gold lobby, a string quartet was playing Bach, as they always did at four o'clock, when people drank afternoon tea and ate cakes and cookies. As Moe listened to the beautiful music he had to remind himself that outside starving people were looking for crusts of bread in garbage bins.

He'd worked hard all through that summer, sending Washington a constant stream of reports. Yet the OSS sent back replies that often didn't make sense, or orders that he knew better than to try to follow. Moe figured that the people sending him new orders were far away from the real war. They didn't know or understand what was going on. Ignoring their orders, he kept traveling in the sweltering heat to find Heisenberg. He interviewed Italian scientists, technicians, engineers—anyone who might know about German or Italian military weapons, machines, and planes. A cable arrived in July from General Donovan telling him he was doing a good job. It made him try all the harder.

On August 21 he received orders telling him that he was still working for the OSS, but that he'd been transferred from the OSS Special Operations to the OSS Technical Section. No explanation was given for the change.

Moe heard bits and pieces of information and gossip about Washington's plans for him. On August 25, the American Seventh Army invaded southern France, and the Free French forces triumphantly rode through the boulevards of Paris to the joyous cheers of Parisians. The people in Washington told Moe to leave Italy and get to Paris. He was to find Marie Curie's son-in-law, the scientist Frederick Joliot-Curie, and interview him and other French scientists about how the Germans were using poison gas and germ warfare. Moe believed Washington was pulling him out of the real dangerous action with assignments that were taking him away from the fighting and from his search for Heisenberg.

Moe learned that after Paris, the OSS planned to send him to Switzerland and maybe even Stockholm. Still more new orders arrived for Moe, but he kept putting them off. Then he heard other secret agents had been sent to France instead of him. In September, he finally left Italy, but not before the Italians recognized the remarkable work that he had done.

To thank Moe for the kindness and courtesy he had shown when he had interviewed the brilliant Italian scientists and their families, Italian president Giuseppe Carnois gave Moe an honorary degree as Doctor of Law from the University of Rome.

This new honor was a great ending to Moe's summer in Italy and his important mission. He agreed to return to London, far away from enemy lines and the risk of being captured. He knew too much about the details of America's top-secret atomic bomb project, and he could be a prize catch for the enemy.

Chapter **15**

The Hunt
for Heisenberg

By September 12, 1944, Moe had arrived in England and reported to the London OSS headquarters. There he learned that earlier that summer, scientists from the Manhattan Project, the U.S. top-secret atomic bomb program, had come to Washington and urged General Groves to find Werner Heisenberg. They were sure the Nazis were depending on Heisenberg's research to build their atomic bomb. Even though Heisenberg's exact location was unknown to them, General Groves and Major Furman thought up a plan. They wanted to persuade Heisenberg to leave Germany and visit Switzerland, a neutral country whose borders were open to both sides fighting the war. Once Heisenberg was in Switzerland, a U.S. agent could find out how much the Germans knew about building the atomic bomb.

119

While Groves and Furman worked out the details of the plan, Moe found a flat and waited for his new orders. He went to shows, concerts, and dinner parties. He had a few dates and wrote long letters to his mother, sister, and brother. He received an $800 raise in salary to $4,600 a year. Mostly, he went to antique book stores to search for old books on languages.

In November, with Paris and Rome liberated, the Allied armies moved toward Germany's main defense —the Siegfried Line. At last, the route into Germany itself seemed open.

But at dawn on Saturday, December 16, 1944, some 250,000 Germans—twenty-five divisions—launched a massive counterattack. The Nazis planned to split the Allied forces in half and drive them all the way back to the sea. Screened by a thick fog along a seventy-five mile front, the Germans caught the United States First Army off guard as they pushed fifteen miles into Allied territory. The Allied line stretched; the armies fell back. This engagement would become known as the Battle of the Bulge.

Meanwhile, Moe waited in London, and then in Paris, until mid-December, when his orders arrived. They had been carefully put together by Donovan and his OSS staff. Years later, Moe told this story about their plan.

The story began with Switzerland's top experimental physicist, Professor Paul Scherr, a secret agent for the United States. Professor Scherr was to invite Heisenberg to give a lecture on December 18, 1944, at the Institute of Technology in Zurich. The OSS hoped that Heisenberg would discuss his research and talk about the German atomic bomb program.

Moe was to go to Switzerland and sit in on that Heisenberg lecture. If Moe thought the German physicist knew too much about making an atomic bomb, Moe was to pull out his gun and shoot to kill Werner Heisenberg.

At the same time Moe was receiving his OSS orders, Werner Heisenberg was getting official Nazi permission to leave Germany. On December 15, 1944, Werner Heisenberg and another German scientist, Carl-Friedrich von Weizsacher, arrived in Zurich. From the moment the Germans arrived in Zurich's spotless train station they were shadowed by OSS agents.

At the Institute, Professor Scherr had left one ticket, reserved for a student, to be picked up on the day of the lecture. The "student" who would call for that ticket would be Moe Berg.

The lecture was supposed to begin at four o'clock. Heisenberg arrived well before that time. Taking Scherr to one side, Heisenberg told the Swiss in private what life was really like in Germany. Most German scientists were kept under close watch by the Gestapo. If they were considered unfriendly to Adolf Hitler, their loved ones disappeared into Nazi concentration camps.

Scherr understood what Heisenberg was talking about. He knew that Germans living in Switzerland were very careful. Everything they said and did was reported directly to Berlin and to the Nazis. Many were terrified that they would be turned over to the Gestapo if they dared to criticize Hitler. Others worried because their children and families were hostages.

Heisenberg talked freely, mixing stories of life in Germany with news of his scientific research.

Heisenberg mentioned some political news. He'd met with Hitler and the Fuhrer was well. Then he told about his experiments. Through it all, he shared gossip about their friends in Germany. Paul Scherr would later report the whole conversation to Moe Berg.

After meeting with Scherr, Heisenberg prepared to give his lecture to the waiting audience. At four o'clock, about two dozen people took seats in the first floor auditorium of the Institute. Some were Heisenberg's friends. Some wore the Nazi uniform with swastika armbands. Some were members of the Gestapo, the German secret police in plain clothes sent to listen and report back on what Heisenberg said. Some were graduate students or professors from the Institute. And one was a six foot "student" no one bothered to question.

By putting on student clothes and changing his appearance with a few artful touches of makeup, Moe looked like a student all over again. From his seat in the second row, he could see everyone in the room. Paul Scherr and Carl Friedrich von Weizsacher sat in front of him. Moe was sure von Weizsacher was a Gestapo agent sent on the trip to report to Berlin on Heisenberg.

Moe watched Heisenberg walk quickly into the room and adjust the blackboard. After he placed the blackboard in a comfortable position, the physicist took out his notes and began to talk, pacing back and forth in front of the room.

Moe did what he usually did in a classroom. He took out his pen and notebook and prepared to take notes. Moe could catch just a little of what Heisenberg was saying, but he understood it wasn't about the bomb at all. Heisenberg did not mention Germany's atomic bomb program or his research on it. Instead he spoke about his new advanced theory of physics. As he listened, Moe took careful notes, not about what Heisenberg was saying, but about how he looked.

Compared to the tall, blond, uniformed Nazis, the Gestapo men, and the other husky Germans in the classroom, Werner Heisenberg appeared small and frail. About five feet six inches, he had reddish blond hair, balding in the back, and bushy eyebrows. Moe thought Heisenberg had sinister eyes. They were both about the same age, but to Moe Heisenberg looked older than his forty-three years.

As the physicist raced on with his lecture, Moe knew that he had to quickly decide what to do next. If he shot Heisenberg he would not get out of the classroom alive.

Listening carefully, Moe tried to decide if Heisenberg was hinting that, with his help, the Germans were close to completing the atomic bomb. But the small, pale man in front of the classroom paced back and forth without mentioning Germany's atomic bomb program. The physicist had begun his lecture by discussing his new advanced theory and had stuck to that topic.

Heisenberg paced and talked. He wrote numbers and equations on the blackboard. Moe took more notes. Outside the Institute the winter light was fading. Time was running out. Heisenberg continued to explain his theory in German. As Moe wrote his notes, he felt the pistol pressing into his chest and grew more certain that this was not the right time to shoot Heisenberg.

Finally, at about 6:30, the lecture was over. The men in the room stood up, stretched and started to talk to each other. Moe went to get his coat. He had brought some gifts for Professor Scherr, which he quietly dropped off at the professor's office. Scherr caught up with Moe and told him that the talk with Heisenberg before the lecture had convinced him that the German scientist was not for Hitler. Scherr believed Heisenberg was not a true Nazi and was unhappy in Germany.

This was just the opening Moe was waiting for. Moe asked Scherr to invite Heisenberg to visit Switzerland once again, but this time with his family. When the Heisenbergs arrived, the OSS would smuggle them out of Switzerland and take them to the United States.

Their brief talk finished, the two returned to the classroom. Heisenberg was still at the blackboard explaining his theory to interested students who lingered after his talk. Moe moved closer, appearing to study the equations on the board, and listened to what Heisenberg was saying. Finally, the auditorium emptied. Heisenberg, the Gestapo officers, and a few others went to dinner at a restaurant near the institute.

While the German physicist sat around the dinner table with his friends, a newsboy, carrying newspapers under his arm, walked through the restaurant, selling his papers from table to table. Heisenberg eagerly bought a newspaper. The Battle of the Bulge was now in its third day. In huge headlines the paper announced that the German armies were pushing back the Allies all the way to Bastogne, a city in Belgium.

Reading the news, Heisenberg announced that the Germans were pulling ahead. To the others at the table he seemed triumphant and gleeful. It was as if he really wanted the Nazis to win. Heisenberg's joy didn't go unnoticed by others. When Moe found out about Heisenberg's remark, he included it in his report to Washington. It would brand Heisenberg as a true Nazi.

A few days after the lecture, Paul Scherr hosted a dinner party in Heisenberg's honor. Moe was invited. Heisenberg had asked all the dinner guests to avoid talking about the war, but feelings were running high. The guests asked Heisenberg about German atrocities against the Jews and the people of the countries Germany had conquered. Heisenberg answered most of the questions by insisting that he was a German, not a Nazi.

Scherr's dinner guests believed that sooner or later Germany was going to lose the war, and they let Heisenberg know their feelings. Heisenberg's reply shocked and surprised the guests. He commented that it would have been good if the Germans had won.

Moe picked up on the scientist's remark. The other guests were angry with Heisenberg for his loyalty to the Nazi cause. But Moe figured out that Heisenberg meant Germany *did not yet have* an atomic bomb ready to use against the Allies or they would have used it. This was the important answer that he had come to Switzerland to learn.

After dinner, Werner Heisenberg walked out into the dimly lit Zurich street. Although the city's lights were on at night, the fuel shortage was keeping the lights burning low. Moe casually left Scherr's house about the same time as Heisenberg. He caught up with the German scientist, making it appear as though he just happened to be walking in the same direction.

Moe couldn't let the man he had been trailing for years just walk out of his life and into the night.

As the pair walked through the snow-covered cobblestone street, Moe did what he always did when he wanted someone to relax, open up and talk to him— he began with small talk. Casually in careful Swiss-German, he asked easy questions about the cold weather, wartime food shortages in Germany, and Heisenberg's trip to Switzerland. Heisenberg returned Moe's questions with polite answers that said nothing.

Moe was walking right next to Werner Heisenberg, the target of his manhunt for almost two years, but he was talking about absolutely nothing that had to do with the atomic bomb. Still casual, but desperately trying to get Heisenberg to open up, Moe persisted. The small, thin, pale man next to him just kept on walking. Then, suddenly, Heisenberg turned off to his hotel, leaving Moe alone on the snowy sidewalk.

Moe quickly pouched his report about Heisenberg to Washington. In it he said that based on what he had seen and heard, he didn't believe the Germans were close to building the atomic bomb. Werner Heisenberg, still alive, returned to Germany and never suspected the plot or Moe.

Later, Moe would find out that Heisenberg had run into trouble when he returned to Germany. The Gestapo was angry with him because he made remarks about Germany losing the war. Heisenberg had been ordered to the Gestapo's Berlin headquarters for questioning, but he had managed to make the Nazis believe he meant no harm and was not putting down the Fatherland.

Moe's report was important to the military experts and the scientists in Washington. Based on Moe's information, the OSS and the atomic scientists believed the Nazis did not have an atomic bomb. The American scientists working on the Manhattan Project were also pleased with Moe's work because it eased the pressure on them. Now the United States did not have to build two atomic bombs to help end the war—one to drop over Germany, the other to drop over Japan—but could concentrate on building one bomb targeted at Japan.

Heisenberg's lecture and his remarks at Scherr's dinner, all reported by Moe, had helped the United States and those heading the Manhattan Project come to this important decision. The President of the United States, especially, was pleased with Moe's work.

But General Groves was upset that Moe had placed himself so close to Heisenberg. If Moe had been discovered and kidnapped by the Gestapo or Nazi secret agents, he might have been forced to spill everything. He couldn't put himself in danger that way or take those kind of chances ever again.

General Groves ordered Moe not to try to follow Heisenberg into Germany and not to get anywhere near the Gestapo or any other Germans in Switzerland. Moe did as he was told and began to work on leads that were much less dangerous—the tone of the general's orders left Moe no choice. He was ordered to remain in Switzerland, where it would be his job to make sure Paul Scherr was happy and that he could be counted on.

That winter in Zurich, Moe saw a lot of Paul Scherr and his family. Moe had discovered a true friend.

Together, the men explored books, history, and philosophy, went skiing, biking, and swimming, and ate wonderful food. Their talk could shift from Greek philosophy to uranium chain reactions to baseball, junk food, and American movies without skipping a beat.

Just as he had with the Ferri children in Italy, Moe quickly became an "uncle" to the Scherr children, playing with them and teaching them baseball. The children thought he was a bodyguard sent by the United States to protect them if the Germans invaded Switzerland and tried to kidnap their father. This story was an easy cover for Moe, and he didn't try to change it.

Even as Moe appeared to be nothing more than a family friend, he and Scherr spied on the Axis. Whatever gossip or news Scherr picked up from German or Japanese scientists or anyone else, he shared with Moe, who insisted that he had to have top priority over any other agent's reports. That way he could send Scherr's information immediately to General Groves.

But with spring, Moe would be on his way again. He received his orders to leave, and the Scherr family became another name on his holiday card list.

Chapter 16

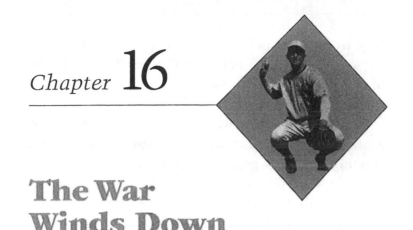

The War
Winds Down

The Army sent a command car and driver to call for Moe in Zurich and drive him through the Alps. With the Scherr episode over, he was on his way to France to meet his boss, General "Wild Bill" Donovan, for breakfast in Paris.

By the spring of 1945, the German armies had retreated from France and General Charles de Gaulle had set up a new government. Moe knew that American secret agents and scientists were right behind the Allied forces pushing toward Berlin. The Alsos team was on the heels of General Patton, scrambling to interview newly captured German scientists and to search their laboratories.

But on the morning Moe and General Donovan sat down for breakfast in a Parisian sidewalk cafe, a news flash from the United States swept through Paris and the world. President Franklin Delano Roosevelt died suddenly on April 12, 1945, of a cerebral hemorrhage at Warm Springs, Georgia.

To Moe, Roosevelt was much more than a president. He was a hero, a strong wartime leader with a glowing vision of peace. General Donovan tried to cheer Moe by telling him that President Roosevelt knew how Moe was helping the United States win the war, but Moe still felt terrible.

Eventually, Moe put his feelings aside and listened as the General told him about his next secret mission. The war was winding down, the General told Moe, but now there were new problems. Donovan wanted Moe to travel behind the victorious Allied troops sweeping through the broken German army lines. He wanted Moe to get to the atomic laboratories hidden in southern Germany. The United States wanted to know the full story behind the German atomic bomb program.

A few days after his breakfast with General Donovan in Paris, Moe flew to Göttingen, in southern Germany. His job was to investigate the famous scientific institute where Paul Scherr and other well-known physicists had trained and done research. After he landed, he traveled through the conquered countryside. As the jeep carried him over the muddy country roads, Moe saw how badly Germany had been beaten.

Allied fighter planes flew low looking for targets to strafe, throwing long shadows over the roads and fields. No German fighter planes took off to intercept them. Frightened German boys, fourteen and fifteen years old, drafted into the army for the final battles, walked the dirt roads, trying to return to their families. Groups of starved people in ragged prisoner uniforms roamed over the fields and woods. They were the slave laborers brought in from conquered countries to work in German factories. Most were running from the Nazi soldiers, trying to find a way to return home. Some soldiers still believed in Hitler and stalked the roads and woods, shooting deserters or hanging them from trees.

As Moe arrived at the physics institute in Göttingen, he caught up with the Alsos team and other scientists and agents from England and France. They had all come together at the secret laboratory at Göttingen. They didn't have to worry about German sniper fire, however. The last organized platoons of German soldiers had cleared out, heading east.

Entering the secret research laboratory, Moe and the other agents stared in disbelief. The question, "Do the Nazis have an atomic bomb?" was finally answered. The Germans had absolutely nothing.

The Germans hadn't stockpiled enough raw materials. They hadn't yet started to produce pure U235, a rare form of uranium. Without U235, there could be no bomb.

All along, the German propaganda about a top-secret bomb program had been a lie. The American atomic scientists had always been far, far ahead of the Nazis.

Still, Moe and the other agents wanted to know more about the secret German research. Was there something they missed? Something more they should know about? But since the conquered German laboratory officially belonged to the U.S. armed forces and Moe was a civilian, he had to stand aside as the military teams took over.

Moe watched as they rummaged through the files, desks, drawers, and trash cans. They inspected the equipment and the machinery and the laboratory apparatus and they looked for supplies of raw materials. While the military searched for clues, Moe went into the small side rooms, listened and took notes as the American military interpreters questioned the captured enemy scientists. Because Moe understood atomic physics better than many of the military investigators, he was allowed to offer ideas for questions, which the army interrogators then asked the Germans.

The Allies were arresting other German scientists all over Germany and Austria. Some still lived near their secret laboratories. Others had tried to hide from the Allies. Moe made lists of the German scientists working on the atomic bomb and told the American officers leading the arrests where they were living so that army platoons could take them into custody.

His list read like a who's who of famous physicists, and included Heisenberg, Weizsacher, Hahn, Laue, Diebner and many other important scientists that students read about in their textbooks.

The United States Army knew there was still more hidden information, but that they would have to search for it because of Werner Heisenberg's actions during the last days before Hitler's surrender. Knowing the Allies were on their way, Heisenberg had ordered his precious supplies—two tons of materials used in the atomic experiments—to be stored in oil drums and hidden in a mill near another secret laboratory. Heisenberg ordered his supply of uranium buried in a field which was then plowed to make it look like a farm. He also ordered his top-secret atomic research papers sealed inside metal drums, which were dropped into a deep pit filled with garbage and slime.

When Heisenberg's laboratory was finally captured, U.S. enlisted men discovered the drums in the cesspool and hauled them up. Once the filthy drums were opened, the smelly papers revealed exactly the same story as the one Moe had found in Göttingen. There had been nothing for the United States to worry about. Heisenberg's research papers proved without a doubt that the German atomic bomb program was only just beginning. Moe's feeling that the Germans did not have the bomb had been right all along.

That April 1945, the newspapers were filled with important bulletins. Soldiers from the United States and the Soviet Union met at the Elbe River, shook hands, and celebrated victory over their common enemy, the Germans. Mussolini had been executed, and his body hung by the heels from a lamppost. Hitler had committed suicide. The end of the war in Europe was in sight.

American troops had also discovered the full horror of Hitler's Germany—the concentration camps, the instruments of torture, and the gas chambers used to kill millions of Jews and other people considered "undesirable" by the Nazis. The United States, determined to punish those responsible for the atrocities, joined with the Soviets, the British, and the French to create an international military tribunal that would put twenty-two high German officials on trial starting in November 1945 and continuing until 1949. While the war was still on, twenty-six nations met in San Francisco to create a new international organization called the United Nations.

April was a turning point in Moe's life as well. Everything Moe had thought about and done for the last three years had to do with finding out about Germany's atomic bomb project. But no one needed to know about it any more. For the time being, no one needed Moe.

Going back to the life he had led before the war was impossible. Moe knew he was far too old to play major league baseball. Besides, Moe had liked his life as a secret agent. He didn't want it to change. Eventually, however, he was ordered to return home.

By the end of April Moe was back in the Roseville section of Newark, New Jersey, with his mother, Rose, and his sister, Ethel. His adoring mother and sister overfed him with rich home cooking, kept him supplied with newspapers from around the world, and breathlessly waited to hear his every whim. Moe waited for his next set of orders. He couldn't wait to get out of the house and get far away from Newark.

Chapter **17**

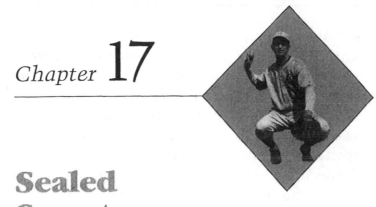

Sealed Secrets

As the war in Europe began to wind down later that spring, Moe got his new orders. A new arms race was building up between the Soviet Union and the United States. Formerly allies, these powers both wanted to capture Nazi physicists and take them back to their own countries. Even though Germany had lost the war, there was a good chance its scientists had discovered some useful information about A-bomb design.

By early May, Moe was on his way back to London on a plane carrying Donovan, his staff, and other members of the OSS. His assignment was to visit Dr. Lise Meitner in Sweden. In 1944, Lise Meitner's two German research partners, Otto Hahn, director of the Kaiser Wilhelm Institute in Berlin, and Fritz Strassmann, had been awarded the Nobel Prize for their discovery of fission. To her great disappointment, Dr. Meitner had been ignored by the Nobel committee, even though she was the first to understand that the nucleus of the atom could be split. She believed that along with her teammates Hahn and Strassmann, she also deserved to be recognized for her important scientific contribution.

It was up to Moe to make friends with this formal woman who seemed part schoolteacher, part older aunt, and who was very precise about everything. His job was to quickly find out how she felt about both the United States and the Soviet Union. Even more, he needed to learn whether there was any chance this brilliant scientist might go to work for the Soviets.

Introducing himself to Dr. Meitner in June, Moe presented her with a letter from Paul Scherr. Actually, it was an invitation from Scherr to come to work in Zurich, at the physics institute. Before long, Dr. Meitner talked to Moe as if she'd known him for years, and as a trusted friend. She would think over Scherr's offer.

Then Moe listened closely as she described how difficult and lonely her life had been during Hitler's rule. Because she was a Jew, the Germans had taken her money, her work, everything. Before the war she had worked with people she trusted. But since Hitler, the very same people had turned their backs on the Jews, and on her. In particular, her former boss, Otto Hahn, had abandoned her.

As she finished talking about her feelings and how alone she felt those past seven years in Sweden, Moe made an offer. Would she like to write to Otto Hahn who was now in the United States? Moe would see to it that Hahn received her letter.

Actually, Otto Hahn was nowhere near the United States. Moe knew that Hahn and the other captured German scientists, including Werner Heisenberg, were being held together in Belgium. Moe was testing Lise Meitner by using the letter as a way to find out how she felt about Otto Hahn and the other German scientists.

Like the rest of the world, Lise Meitner had learned about the horrors and atrocities committed by Germany while Hitler was in power. In her letter to Otto Hahn, Lise Meitner told him she was angry with him for doing research for Adolf Hitler. She wondered how Hahn could have worked for the Nazis and never protested against their actions.

Moe carried the letter out of her house, and out of Sweden. But the letter did not go to Otto Hahn, or even to Belgium. It found its way to General Groves in Washington. Months later, Meitner learned from a British agent that Otto Hahn had never received the letter. Lise Meitner was angry with Moe—but not for long. They met just once after that in early January of the next year. By the time they parted Moe had managed to convince her that he meant well. Once again, they were good friends. Though he knew people just as famous, Lise Meitner would always be special to him, someone he really cared about. He loved to tell stories of his stay in Stockholm and his summer visits with Dr. Meitner.

On August 6, 1945, after repeatedly warning the Japanese to surrender, the United States dropped a single atomic bomb on the city of Hiroshima, Japan, at exactly 8:15 A.M. When the Japanese government continued to refuse to surrender, the United States dropped a second atomic bomb over Nagasaki.

The information that Moe had carefully guarded for years was spilled over the front pages of every newspaper in the world. The atomic bomb was no longer a secret. In the months following the atomic bomb explosions, Moe realized that he was no longer needed to guard this important secret. He began to see signs that the people at the OSS in Washington didn't think of him as useful any more.

As he traveled between Zurich, London, Rome and finally the United States, Moe began to feel uneasy about the OSS cables that followed him. For the first time, there were cables asking him how he was spending OSS funds, demanding to know what he was doing with the money from his expense account. The government had never questioned him before, but now his supervisors asked why he was staying at the most expensive hotels, eating at the best restaurants, and traveling first class.

Moe had always lived this way, especially when he was on assignment. No one had ever seemed to mind before. As the cables came in, he brushed them aside, but his bosses didn't stop questioning how he spent his money. The OSS officials insisted that he write down everything he spent, then explain where and why he spent the government money. There were new forms for him to fill out. But filling out those long, tiresome forms just wasn't his style. He put them off.

There were new people running the OSS office in Washington. Moe began to worry whether the new bosses were impressed with him. Did they like him? Were they choosing someone else for the top-secret jobs that had once been his alone? He tormented himself with the idea that the new people at the OSS didn't know enough about him and didn't understand how he operated.

When he wanted to feel better he reminded himself that there were still stories about him in the newspapers. Reporters liked to tell about the unknown Jewish kid from Newark who played baseball, graduated from Princeton, and had lasted in the majors for thirteen seasons. People still talked about Moe's appearances on the radio show, *Information Please.* He still knew movie stars, and other important world-famous people.

Although Moe still told a lot of good and funny stories about his great baseball days, he realized that the past didn't mean as much anymore. People were more interested in stories about the war that had just ended. Moe knew he would never be able to tell the whole exciting truth about his own heroic war adventures because they would be forever classified top-secret. Moe had taken an oath never to tell. And he would never break his word.

By 1946, peace had brought in a new, strange unrest between the United States and the Soviet Union. The politicians and statesmen from the two countries were growing more and more suspicious of one another. Soviet, British, and American agents raced each other into the liberated German territory to capture Nazi scientists, taking them into "protective custody."

Moe's new job was to track down the scientists still left in Europe and to find out what the Soviets were offering them. If possible, the Americans would try to beat the Soviet offer. Quietly traveling between Germany, France, England, Sweden, the Netherlands, and

Switzerland, Moe asked questions, took notes, and followed leads. He found out how much atomic information the scientists had and met with world famous researchers. From that autumn until the following February, he appeared and disappeared all over Europe.

While the world was changing around him, Moe had to face one of the biggest changes of all in his own life. Because the war was over, President Harry S. Truman reasoned that the United States didn't need its spy network any longer, and he signed an order closing down the OSS After October 1, the OSS would become the Strategic Services Unit (SSU), headed by Brigadier General John Magruder, who had been OSS Special Warfare Chief.

Moe learned that his powerful friends were going to resign from the OSS. Its chief, "Wild Bill" Donovan, and Howard Dix, head of the OSS Technical Section, told him they were going back to their families and to their careers. And yet, before he left, Howard Dix loyally tried to help Moe. He asked Moe to write about his exploits—to put down on paper all the episodes he'd lived through for the OSS. Dix felt this would help the new staff at SSU to understand Moe's important part in helping the United States win the war. But Moe found it difficult to share this information with the new staff.

At the same time that his old friends were asking him to write about his outstanding work, newly hired government officials were hounding him. They were demanding to know how he had spent over $20,000 of OSS money during a two-year assignment. They couldn't understand why Moe had always avoided filling out forms and failed to send in his expense account records. In the past, headquarters had let him get away with this, but the new SSU people wouldn't allow him to put them off any longer.

Still, Moe wasn't used to taking orders and he didn't want to be pushed around. By February, Moe thought it was time for a vacation. Skiing seemed like a good idea. There was no need to tell anyone where he was going, or when he would be back. He never did. Maybe he would try to write the story of what he did during the war. In the meantime, the Swiss Alps were where he wanted to be, and skiing was what he wanted to do. So he put everything on hold, and dropped out of sight.

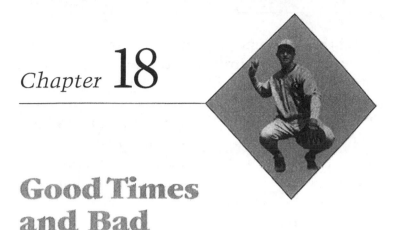

Chapter **18**

Good Times
and Bad

Moe couldn't disappear forever. Even though he knew better than anyone else where to search out hostile scientists and their secrets, Moe couldn't travel around Europe as he pleased any longer. Every time he stopped at the London office, the SSU told him to return to the United States. Moe didn't have a choice anymore. His new instructions from Washington were loud and clear: tell us how you spent our money.

The SSU kept hounding him for his overdue records and late reports. Moe didn't like it one bit. No one had ever treated him this way before. In the past, he had never bothered filling out forms. He always had much better things to do.

Yet the very same time one part of the U.S. government was giving him a hard time, another part was offering him an award, a medal for his outstanding work as a spy during the war. His old boss, Howard Dix, had been pushing the government to give Moe the Medal of Freedom. This medal, first awarded in 1945, was given by the United States government to recognize a person's outstanding contribution to the war effort through acts performed outside the United States. Usually, the award carried an explanation, telling why the person had earned the honor. Moe's work was classified top-secret and all his records were locked away. Not even his ex-boss could tell why Moe should be awarded the medal.

Even so, in early October 1945, Moe was awarded the coveted Medal of Freedom. The medal didn't describe any of Moe's heroic acts or exploits. The citation simply said:

In a position of responsibility in the European Theater, he exhibited analytical abilities and a keen planning mind. He inspired both respect and constant high level of endeavor on the part of his subordinates, which enabled his section to produce studies and analyses vital to the mounting of the American operations.

Moe was proud of the very high honor. But he also had mixed feelings about the award. He hated the way the government insisted on his overdue expense accounts. He was annoyed that they kept nagging him for his day-to-day work reports. Besides, he had sworn never to tell about his exploits as a secret agent. He had taken an oath.

In early December, he decided to turn down the honor. Without giving a reason he returned the medal to the United States government. He realized that returning it would always puzzle everyone, yet he wouldn't explain his actions, except to say that the medal embarrassed him.

With the war over, the people who had worked with Moe began to leave the SSU, eager to return to their homes and families once again. But Moe didn't have any other life he wanted to go back to. He didn't like working nine to five as a lawyer in an office. He didn't want to become a teacher or a college professor. He loved his life as a secret agent; he loved traveling around the world, meeting people, and working on thrilling assignments. He didn't want anything to change.

But the war was finished; the government no longer needed as many secret agents. The phone calls from Washington became less and less frequent. There weren't any more exciting assignments. Once in a while, Moe was invited to lunches, parties, or dinners by old teammates, friendly scientists, or ex-government agents. But there was no real work for him to do.

His days became quiet and uninterrupted. Moe had always liked to study. Now he began to search out answers to questions about languages as he had done years earlier at Princeton and the Sorbonne.

But without a job or a paycheck, Moe could no longer afford to live in first-rate hotels, eat in the finest restaurants, enjoy the most expensive wines, or wear new suits. Before long he faced the hard facts. He had no money to finance the lifestyle that he loved; he had to return to Newark, New Jersey.

After arriving at Newark's Penn Station in 1947, Moe took a bus to his brother's house. He had no other choice but to move in with his older brother,

Dr. Samuel Berg, now a successful dermatologist. It was tolerable for Moe only because he thought the living arrangement would be for a very short while. He was sure that soon there would be a phone call from the SSU asking him to rush back to Washington. Then, he would be out of Sam's house and on his way to another mysterious, special assignment. While waiting for that phone call, Moe stayed in shape. He walked and ran with Sam on the cinder paths of nearby Branch Brook Park.

Returning GIs were scrambling to find peacetime jobs, but Moe wasn't ready to earn a living in the usual way. He did not try to find work as a lawyer or as a teacher. He even turned down a coaching job with the White Sox and refused an offer from Ted Williams and his old Boston team, the Red Sox. Instead, Moe waited for that one important phone call from the SSU. Deep down, even though it was 1945 and the war was over, Moe believed the SSU needed him to get the inside story on the Soviets.

By 1951, Moe was facing some serious money troubles. He owed back taxes to the government, as a result of a bad business investment made years earlier. The Internal Revenue Service asked for more than $7,500 plus 6 percent interest for every year that the taxes had not been paid. A person could buy a large house for much less. Moe offered to pay back all that he could afford, but the IRS didn't think the offer was enough.

Despite his trouble, Moe enjoyed studying again and hunting down little known information about languages. Libraries and antique bookstores were free and full of fascinating facts. He spent hours browsing the shelves for rare books. While he waited for Washington to call, he filled notebooks with lists and wrote notes to himself about odd people. He made notes about how to write better reports and how best to tell the facts about a new discovery. He also made many proposals for secret assignments to the SSU. If they couldn't think up an assignment for him, he would provide the ideas. He still considered himself an agent who could uncover hidden facts and help his country.

One year slowly melted into another. Moe continued to wear his black tie, white nylon shirt and dark suit, but his clothes were a little ragged, even threadbare. Moe began to look less like the fit athlete in top shape and more like a middle aged man, his dark suit jacket a little too tight to be buttoned comfortably. Instead of traveling on top-secret assignments, he visited friends in Manhattan, Boston, and Washington, and attended ball games and scientific meetings. He had never learned to drive a car, and he wouldn't tell how he managed to get around. It was something he just didn't want to talk about.

Moe was always a clever storyteller with wonderful adventures and sports yarns. When he showed up, his friends welcomed him. Sometimes he stayed a night or a weekend, sometimes weeks or even months. After he ran out of stories, he packed his small gym bag and disappeared.

Between visits to friends he went back to Sam's house, although the two brothers weren't getting along. Sam complained about the growing mountains of newspapers Moe carried into the house every day.

147

He was angry because newspapers spilled over from Moe's upstairs bedroom to the downstairs dining room and living room; they lay piled in corners, on chairs, tables—everywhere. Moe didn't allow Sam to touch his papers. If Sam picked up and read a newspaper before Moe opened it, Moe got upset.

It was a relief for both brothers when the Central Intelligence Agency finally called Moe with an assignment. The CIA had taken over the SSU. Once again the reason for the call was a secret concerning a possible threat to the United States.

By 1950, many Americans were gripped with fears about the Soviet Union and its communist government. Senator Joseph McCarthy from Wisconsin had convinced the country that hidden communists were living in the United States.

Two years earlier Moe had proposed that he go to Europe, hunt up the atomic scientists he met during the war, and find out what they knew about Soviet atomic research. The CIA asked Moe to renew his contacts with the European atomic researchers he had met during war.

Moe couldn't wait to get to Europe and begin his hunt.

While he planned the trip, he dreamed of eating in the best restaurants, living in the finest hotels, and going where he pleased.

But Moe soon discovered that it wasn't like old times. He could no longer do as he pleased. The CIA insisted on new rules. Even so, Moe continued to ignore their instructions. Unlike the new agents, he didn't keep a list of what he was doing from one day to the next. He didn't bother to check in regularly at the CIA headquarters in London, Paris, or Berne. When he did appear, he was close-mouthed, revealing nothing about his activities or plans. If only Washington left him alone to sniff out a lead or follow up his hunch, he would come up with lots of information. But how could he accomplish anything if he had to spend his time writing reports and answering lots of questions? Besides, how he managed to get his information was his own personal secret.

In spite of the CIA's questions and protests, Moe moved quickly and quietly throughout Europe. More important, he also knew how to get people to relax and tell him what he had come to learn. He saw old friends who were scientists, mainly in Germany, England, and Italy. Usually, he appeared without warning. Often he was invited to important dinners and parties. Sometimes he stayed for days or weeks. Then he disappeared without a trace.

As he traveled, Moe found all of Europe dividing itself into two camps—either for the United States or for the Soviet Union. His job was to find out which scientists favored the Soviets and which researchers were loyal to the United States. As usual, he asked questions and made lists of names, addresses, and laboratories. He put together bits and pieces of information, tracked down leads, and followed up clues. He was always easygoing and friendly as he tried to get the inside story.

But Moe soon discovered he was not uncovering any startling facts or new, important information. After visiting a handful of scientists in Switzerland, England, and Germany, he didn't have any secrets or fresh news to give to the people who had hired him. It certainly was not like the old days. It didn't take long to go through his expense account either. After only a few months, the contract for his assignment was over. Moe had to return to Washington.

At CIA headquarters, Moe stepped into a world filled with people who practiced regularity, exactness, and clockwork precision. Moe didn't want to deal with their rules and regulations. At a briefing, Moe described that last trip and tried his best to make his listeners understand why his adventures and information were important. The CIA officials listened politely. Some asked respectful questions. But Moe saw that most were not impressed. Some hinted that he had found nothing important in Europe but wasn't able to admit it.

No one suggested a new assignment or mentioned more work for him.

The train ride from Washington, D.C., to Penn Station, Newark, was only about three and one-half hours, but that journey took Moe out of the world of the secret agents and put him back in a world he had always tried to escape. As Moe rode the escalator down from the train platform to Newark's bustling main station concourse, he knew he was facing the future without a real plan.

Returning to Sam's house, Moe found his mail filled with angry letters from the CIA insisting he fill out his expense account sheets and report how he spent their money. More CIA questionnaires and forms arrived every day. But Moe couldn't be bothered with the details of keeping reports or expense records. Why couldn't the CIA understand?

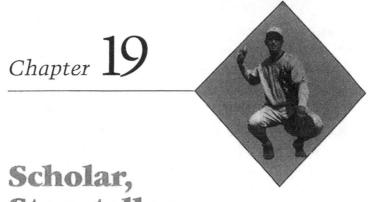

Chapter 19

Scholar, Storyteller

The years 1953 and 1954 melted for Moe into a blur of bookstores, libraries, baseball games, and visits to friends, but there were no assignments from the CIA.

Moe never stopped hoping. He trained every day, running miles in his sweatsuit, and he kept his spy notebooks up to date, filled with ideas and new proposals. But he realized the new organization was not like the friendly, rule-breaking crowd of the good old days.

In the sixties, Moe continued to devote himself to studying languages. But as the days and weeks passed, Moe found that he had more and more empty hours to fill. Often, he read his newspaper from front to back at a lunch counter while he sipped coffee. Sometimes, he talked to waiters going off duty or to elevator operators. He talked to his old OSS buddies or their wives. If acquaintances wondered how he earned money or what he did with his time, Moe dropped hints that he was on a special assignment. When someone younger did not know him, he would gently remind the person that he was the major league baseball player who had astounded the radio public with his answers on *Information Please.*

With the war long over, Moe felt it was now all right to hint that he had once been a secret agent. Moe would drop clues, but stop short of actually telling exactly what he had done in the great war. Always a loner, Moe found it easy to slip in and out of people's lives. He stayed long enough to tell the stories he knew they wanted to hear—stories that made him out to be a hero—then quietly disappeared again.

Sometimes he visited scientists at the Institute for Advanced Studies at Princeton. Other times he stayed with Red Sox or other major league players, lovers of baseball, or retired OSS agents. People were always glad to see him and listen to his stories.

It was his habit now to travel light. He carried a toothbrush, a white nylon shirt, underwear, a pad, and a book as he moved from place to place. If he was a visitor, Moe would wash out his underwear and shirt, and hang them to dry in a bathroom while the family slept. Then he would take down his laundry before anyone got up in the morning and wear the damp clothes to breakfast.

As the days went on, when not in a book store or a library, he searched out people who would take time out of their working days to listen to him, or maybe lend him some money. People would invite him to move in for a while. While his brother Sam treated sick patients and his sister Ethel taught kindergarten, Moe floated in and out of their lives, coming to dinner or moving in for a bit, and just as easily melting into the shadows and disappearing again.

On January 6, 1957, their mother, Rose, died. Moe knew that she went peacefully. Rose had lived her long life just as she wanted to. Although he would miss her, Moe accepted her death.

His older brother was getting fed up with Moe's piles of yellowing newspapers filling his house. The brothers were angry and their arguments grew worse. When Dr. Sam repaid money Moe had borrowed, Moe didn't pay much attention. If his older brother wanted to clear up his debt, Moe allowed him to do it. Finally, in 1964, Sam told Moe he had had enough. After almost seventeen years of putting up with Moe's odd ways, Sam told Moe it was time for him to leave his house.

Moe had no one but Ethel to turn to. A small truck carried his papers and clothes and other belongings and deposited them on Ethel's front porch—just a few blocks away from Sam's house. Moe was too proud to discuss the change, but it was a sweet victory for Ethel. His sister loved two things more than anything else in the world. One was her garden and the other was her kid brother, Moe.

As soon as Moe moved in, he quickly disappeared. Moe feared Ethel would fatten him with her rich cooking or smother him with her kindness, her nagging questions, and her devoted attention. As often as he could, he stayed away. He returned to his sister only when he ran out of money, or when people were tired of putting up with him, and he had absolutely nowhere else to go.

Days, weeks, months, and years went by. Moe's black wavy hair was gray now. His face was more lined, his big body was filled out, and his shoulders sagged forward. Still, there was a dignity about him

Moe loved to tell stories about his adventures. *(Photo courtesy of AP/Wide World Photos.)*

154

when he entered a room, as if he expected everyone to stand up and applaud, or at the very least, to notice his arrival.

By now the thousands of miles he had walked and climbed were beginning to tell. He wore thick-soled black, wide-toed policeman's shoes for his aching feet. When he walked around the city he still moved as if he were stalking someone on a secret mission, looking to the left, to the right, and behind him.

As the years wore on, Moe created his own world of rules to live by. He sent birthday cards to the famous people he knew. He collected matchbooks and menus from famous restaurants. He was proud of the programs from scientific meetings he had attended and the famous scientists he knew by first name who often were the speakers at the events. He treasured his lifetime press card, which gave him free admission to ballparks in Princeton, Chicago, Boston, and Washington.

People treated him with respect when he made an appearance, but he never let them get too close. That's the way Moe wanted it. He spent hours telling stories about the great major league baseball games. He wove together the important plays in baseball and the momentous events of World War II. He loved to hint how he had been an ace undercover agent for the government. If interrupted in the middle of a story even once, however, he would stop, stare, get up, stomp out, and never return.

Moe always carried his little black book of unlisted private telephone numbers that he had collected over the years. It included the numbers for many famous people, including Albert Einstein, Antonio Ferri,

Jimmy Doolittle, Nelson Rockefeller, and Ted Williams. He would call one of them and get through when few others could.

Moe still didn't drive a car. He always traveled by foot, walking miles. Though Moe was never afraid—he'd faced up to many dangers—he was now much older. It was easier for Moe to stay in Ethel's house, reading his newspapers and books. Sometimes he would sit on Ethel's porch, which was surrounded with spectacular trees, bushes, vegetables, and flowers. When he did leave her house, it became an important event instead of a routine trip, as in the old days. Sometimes he took the train to Princeton's Firestone Library or to baseball games, where he used his press pass, or he showed up at scientific meetings as a guest. All those years, even though he didn't have an ordinary everyday job, Moe continued to work on what to him—and to a few college professors—was important research into the history of language.

In May 1972, while staying at Ethel's house, Moe fell out of bed, hitting his head on a night table. After she finally got him to tell her what had happened, Ethel rushed Moe to the hospital. The doctors examined Moe carefully. He was not only suffering from the fall out of bed and his bruises, but from a serious heart condition. While Moe made small talk with the nurses, the doctors broke the news to Ethel.

Two days later, on May 29, 1972, Moe asked a young pretty nurse, "How are the Mets doing today?" The man who had loved baseball years earlier as a kid, had asked his last question about a baseball game. Before she could answer, Moe was gone.

Now the stories Moe loved to tell about baseball and the war would be told by others. As long as there is a baseball fan who loves the game and the characters in it, and as long as someone loves to tell spy stories of World War II, there will always be a tall tale about Moe Berg.

Important Dates in Moe Berg's Life

1897   Moe's parents, Rose Tasker and Bernard Berg, marry.

1898   Older brother Samuel Berg is born.

1900   Sister, Ethel Berg, is born.

1902   Morris "Moe" Berg is born on March 2, 1902.

1918   Graduates from Barringer High School in Newark, New Jersey.

1919   Enters Princeton University.

1923   Graduates from Princeton University.

1923   Joins the Brooklyn Dodgers.

1923–24   Spends the baseball off-season in Paris, France, studying at the Sorbonne.

1924–25   Plays in the Minors.

1926–30   Plays for the Chicago White Sox.

1929   Nominated for Most Valuable Player in the American League.

1930   Earns a Law Degree from Columbia University Law School.

1930	Joins the Manhattan law firm of Satterlee and Canfield.
1931	Sold to the Cleveland Indians.
1932	Traded to the Washington Senators. Plays for the Senators in the 1932, 1933, and 1934 seasons.
1932	First trip to Japan. Travels from Japan to India and China and to the USA.
1933	Member of the Senators American League pennant-winning team.
1934	Sets an American League record by catching in 117 consecutive games without making an error, from 1931 to 1934 for Chicago, Cleveland and Washington.
1934	Goes to Japan with an "All Star Team," which includes Babe Ruth, Connie Mack, Lou Gehrig, and Lefty Gomez.
1934	Takes railroad journey from Asia to Europe.
1935–39	Player and coach for Boston Red Sox.
1938	Appears on *Information Please*, a national radio quiz program.
1942	Moe's father dies on January 14th, the same day Moe announces that he is retiring from baseball.
1942	In February, makes a speech in Japanese to the people of Japan, asking for peace.
1942	Begins "Goodwill" tour of Central and South America on August 22, reporting to Nelson Rockefeller on the political situation.
1942	Becomes a member of the OSS.
1943	Spends summer behind Nazi lines in Yugoslavia.
1943	Joins Project Larson.
1944	Begins search for Italian scientists in May. Finds important secret information hidden in Italy, which he sends to the USA. Receives honorary degree, Doctor of

Law, from the University of Rome. Starts his hunt for Heisenberg.

1944 Attends Heisenberg lecture in Zurich in December. Decides that Heisenberg has not finished building an atomic bomb for Germany. Sends important secret information about other Axis scientists to USA. Convinces U.S. military and scientists that Germany does not have an A-bomb.

1946 Awarded Medal of Freedom, which he later returns to U.S. Government.

1946 Returns to Newark, New Jersey from overseas. Moves in with brother, Dr. Sam Berg.

1952 New CIA assignment in Europe to find out about the atomic weapons in the Soviet Union.

1957 Moe's mother, Rose Berg, dies peacefully.

1963 Moves in with sister, Ethel Berg.

1960–72 Enjoys recalling the "Moe Berg" legend.

1972 Moe dies on May 29 at the Clara Maas Medical Center in Belleville, New Jersey.

Bibliography

Allen, George R. "The Strange Story of Moe Berg, Athlete, Scholar, Spy." Pamphlet, speech given for the William J. White Dinner of the Franklin Inn Club, Philadelphia, January 17, 1991.

Berg, Ethel. *My Brother, Morris Berg: The Real Moe.* Newark, NJ: private publisher, 1976.

Burns, Ken, producer and writer. *When It Was a Game.* A historical documentary film about baseball, 1994.

Cunningham, John T. *Newark.* Newark, NJ: New Jersey Historical Society, 1966, revised 1988.

Daley, Arthur. "Moe Berg, a Man of Many Facets." *New York Times,* June 1, 1972.

Daley, Arthur. "Right Man, Wrong Time." *New York Times,* December 2, 1964.

Dawidoff, Nicholas. *The Catcher Was a Spy: The Mysterious Life of Moe Berg.* New York: Pantheon, 1994.

Goldberg, Hy. "Moe Berg: A Man of Many Talents." *Newark Evening News,* June 1, 1972.

Grey, Vivian. *The Invisible Giants: Atoms, Nuclei and Radioisotopes.* Boston: Little, Brown, 1970.

Grey, Vivian. *Secret of the Mysterious Rays: The Discovery of Nuclear Energy.* New York: Basic Books, 1969.

Hotchner, A.E. *Papa Hemingway.* New York: Bantam, 1967.

Kaufman, Louis, Barbara Fitzgerald, and Tom Sewell. *Moe Berg: Athlete, Scholar, Spy.* Boston: Little, Brown, 1974.

Leuchtenberg, William E., editor. *Time-Life History of the United States.* Vol. 2, *New Deal and Global War.* New York: Time Incorporated, 1964.

Leuchtenberg, William E., editor. *Time-Life History of the United States*. Vol. 12, *The Great Age of Change*. New York: Time Incorporated, 1964.

Powers, Thomas. *Heisenberg's War*. New York: Knopf, 1993.

Ribalow, Harold U., and Z. Meir. *The Jew in American Sports*. New York: Hippocrene Books, 1985.

Shepley, James R., and Clair Blair, Jr. *The Hydrogen Bomb: The Men, the Menace, the Mechanism*. New York: David McKay, 1954.

Williams, Bob. "Doctor Doolittle's Death Recalls the Tokyo Raid," *Trowel* magazine, Grand Lodge of Masons in Massachusetts, spring 1994.

Zborowski, Mark, and Elizabeth Herzog. *Life is With People: The Culture of the Shtetl*. New York: Schocken Paperback, 1952.

Index

Page numbers in *italics* refer to photographs.

165

166

168

CPSIA information can be obtained
at www.ICGtesting.com
Printed in the USA
LVHW091820180719
624481LV00002BA/273/P

9 780827 606203